Chicana/o Identity in a Changing U.S. Society

T0163484

THE MEXICAN AMERICAN EXPERIENCE

Adela de la Torre, EDITOR

Other books in the series:

Mexican Americans and Health: ¡Sana! ¡Sana!
  Adela de la Torre and Antonio L. Estrada

Chicano Popular Culture: Que Hable el Pueblo
  Charles M. Tatum

Mexican Americans and the U.S. Economy: Quest for Buenos Días
  Arturo González

Mexican Americans and the Law:
¡El Pueblo Unido Jamás Será Vencido!
  Reynaldo Anaya Valencia, Sonia R. García, Henry Flores,
  and José Roberto Juárez Jr.

Chicana/o Identity in a Changing U.S. Society

¿Quién Soy? ¿Quiénes Somos?

by Aída Hurtado and Patricia Gurin

The University of Arizona Press   Tucson

The University of Arizona Press
© 2004 The Arizona Board of Regents
All rights reserved
www.uapress.arizona.edu

⊜ This book is printed on acid-free, archival-quality paper.
Manufactured in the United States of America

11 15 14 13 12 11 10 6 5 4 3 2

Library of Congress Cataloging-in-Publication Data

Hurtado, Aída.
Chicana/o identity in a changing U.S. society : ¿quién soy? ¿quiénes somos? /
by Aída Hurtado and Patricia Gurin.
p. cm. — (Mexican American experience)
Includes bibliographical references (p.   ) and index.
ISBN 0-8165-2205-7 (paper : alk. paper)
1. Mexican Americans. I. Gurin, Patricia. II. Title. III. Series.
E184.M5H865 2004
305.868'72073—dc22
2003023447

Publication of this book is made possible in part by the proceeds of a permanent
endowment created with the assistance of a Challenge Grant from the National
Endowment for the Humanities, a federal agency.

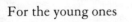

For the young ones

■ CONTENTS

List of Figures ix
Table ix
Acknowledgments xi
Introduction xiii
    A Word about Our Perspective xviii

1. *¿Quién Soy?:* The Development of Self 3

The Development of a Positive Sense of Self: Ethnicity, Race, Class,
    and Gender 6
Conclusions: Multiple Social Adaptations to Cultural
    Transformations 22
Summary 24
    Discussion Exercises 25

2. *¿Quiénes Somos?:* The Importance of Social Identity 27

Personal Identity and Social Identity 30
The Creation of Social Identities 36
Identification and Consciousness in Ethnic Identity Formation 50
An Example of Identification and Consciousness 51
Summary 64
    Discussion Exercises 66

3. Language, Culture, and Community: Group Life in Creating and
Maintaining Identities 68

Meritocracy 69
Universal Rule 69
Degrouping 73
Regrouping through Empowerment 81
Reclamaciones: Toward a Whole Self 85
Regrouping the Degrouped Group 105
Summary 107
    Discussion Exercises 108
    Notes 108

4. Conclusions: The Future of Identity Formations 109

Multiple Social Adaptations to Cultural Transformations 112

New Developments in the Study of Social Identities:
Transnationalism and Transculturalism 114
Summary 126
Discussion Exercises 127
Note 128

Glossary 129
Bibliography 135
Source Credits 141
Index 145

■ LIST OF FIGURES

1. María Hurtado conducting a Cara y Corazón workshop 5
2. Assimilation model 10
3. Kurt Lewin's concept of life space 14
4. Theoretical developments in the study of ethnic identity 14
5. An individual's life space 15
6. Social identity altar built by Dr. Sandra Pacheco 28
7. Amalia Mesa-Bains's altar to Dolores del Río 29
8. Commonalities in social identities and differences in personal identities 36
9. Birth congratulations cards showing marked gender differences 41
10. Cropped images of a man and a woman 41
11. The conceptual difference between personal and social identities 55
12. *Tamalada,* by Carmen Lomas Garza 104
13. *Posada,* by Carmen Lomas Garza 105
14. *Homenaje a Frida Kahlo,* by Yreina D. Cervántez 106
15. *Time* magazine cover for "Amexica" special issue 110
16. Negative versus positive cultural adaptations distributed along a normal curve 114
17. Relative increase in positive, and decrease in negative, cultural adaptations 115
18. "The Border Is Everywhere" map of Latino/a population distribution 118

■ TABLE

1. Northern California High Schools and the Availability of Advanced Placement Courses 72

■ ACKNOWLEDGMENTS

We are grateful to our research assistants, whose hard work and critical insights made this book infinitely better: Lakeya Cherry, Shane Fisher, Nadia Grosfoguel, Janelle Silva, Renae Olivas, Mrinal Sinha, and Jessica Vázquez. We also thank Arcelia Hurtado, whose "eagle eyes" and critical mind clarified many of the ideas in this book.

We also acknowledge the following people from the University of Arizona Press: Adela de la Torre, whose brilliant foresight created this entire book series; Patti Hartmann, whose invaluable guidance brought this book to fruition; and Kirsteen E. Anderson, whose fine-tuning brought clarity and crispness to the manuscript.

Last and foremost we acknowledge our respective families as they go through many of the identity transitions we explore in this book. Aída thanks Craig, Erin, Matt, Chanel, Bonnie, Arcelia, Pepe, and Mom. Pat thanks Jerry, Jennifer, Chloe, and Bryan.

■ INTRODUCTION

¿Quién soy yo? (Who am I?)

The truth is that I am more than
What I appear to be today.

No one realizes that I am the four-year-old
who my mother took with her *una noche*
to find her father with *otra mujer*—
their yells, my father's fist, my mother's hysterical tears
Still I felt nothing, did nothing
Just wanting it to stop.
I learned not to feel, not to get too close.

No one knows that I am the little girl who had open
sores all over her still forming
body, her mother wondering if it was
all those sodas I drank with sugar
only to discover one dark night
that bed bugs were sucking blood
from my legs, my arms.
Y mi mamá asustada burning the
mattress that so well hid the culprits that
were abusing my body for their pleasure.

¿Quién soy yo?

No one really knows that I am
The young girl who wanted nothing
More than a pair of moccasins
For her sixth birthday.
They seemed to be such
An extravagant purchase at the time.
It was the time we lived
In a two-room shack with an outhouse.
It was a time that I had for so long
cleverly blocked from my memory—
El dolor, the pain, numbs the senses.
It was the time my mamá had

una escuelita where for
fifty cents a week she would teach
chicanitos y chicanitas how to spell, read,
add, and subtract—*mi primer educación*.

¿Quién soy yo?

I am the junior high student
who ate lunch for 25 cents a day.
Y un día mi mamá said, *"Tienes que
ser fuerte. Como las meras mujeres."*
She had no money for
lunch that day.
Aprendí ser fuerte. I learned to be strong.

¿Quién soy yo?

I am the high school student
Who didn't get invited to the senior prom
Because she was unattractive,
Unlike the girls who easily found their
way into school clubs and organizations
not for what they knew, but how they looked.
The girl who was told by the sponsor
of the Future Teachers of America that
she would never be a teacher because
she had an "F" in chemistry.
"Teachers don't make F's," she said.
She didn't know that I had sprained my knee
so badly I could not walk to school for weeks.
But there was no money to see the doctor
Nomás no había dinero—this was
Just the way it was. . . .
Just like when I was three years old
and fell hard on the pavement

Knocked out cold with a concussion—
But no hospital, no medication
Just a doctor's house call.

¿Quién soy yo?

I am the woman who decided that
mis hijos, if I had them, would
never have to endure *el dolor.*
I am the *mujer* Chicana who endured
an abusive marriage because that was just the
nature of how things were in Laredo.
*"Todos los hombres son iguales. Me
voy a vengar de todos los hombres,"*
decía mi mamá—a victim of despair and
dysfunctional relationships.
I learned closeness led to *violencia.*

¿Quién soy yo?

I am the graduate student who left Laredo
To take the risks my parents were afraid of,
The Chicana at the University of Michigan
Filled with awe at the sheer fact
that I was there; knowing full well
mi familia did not understand what I
was doing or where I was going,
writing *"ese libro que parece que
nunca va a terminar."*
"Que te crees tu," mi mamá
had said to me in junior high
when I told her I wanted to go
to college—
"El colegio es para los ricos."

It was then, in junior high that
I began not to heed her message—
Where my identity began to evolve
around the idea that I could be separate
But that I would have to take the risks
of being "different" to my *familia* and to
mi raza en Laredo.

¿Quién soy yo?

Soy la mujer
Haunted by childhood memories

Buried deep in my subconscious
Appearing to me in dreams of evil spirits
Wanting to penetrate
mi cuerpo
Terrorizing my trembling body
at night unable to sleep
I am involved with someone I shouldn't.
My memory never lets me forget the
perils of closeness.

¿Quién soy yo?
I am a multiplicity of identities
That frighten me, guard me, teach me
Love me.

—Laura Rendón, 2000

Professor Rendón in her poem *"Quién soy yo?"* (Who am I?) poses the question of who she is as a person. She sees herself as smart but unappreciated by some of her teachers, as a risk taker who goes away to graduate school, and as a survivor. Social psychologists call these self-perceptions **personal identity.** Henri Tajfel (1981) and others define personal identity as an aspect of self composed of psychological traits and dispositions that give us personal uniqueness. Personal identity is derived from intrapsychic influences, many of which are socialized within families. From this perspective, human beings have a great deal in common precisely because our personal identities contain certain universal processes such as loving, mating, raising children, and doing productive work. These activities are universal components of how we define who we are. Personal identity is relatively stable and coherent over time. In chapter 1, *"¿Quién Soy?: The Development of Self,"* we address how individuals develop a positive sense of who they are as people. We look at the various socialization influences that affect their development of self. In particular, we look at family, schools, and community. It is within these contexts that individuals develop their sense of who they are.

Professor Rendón also includes in her definition of self many of the groups she belongs to. She is a "Chicana" who comes from a working-class background, who lived in "a two-room shack with an outhouse," and in whose family "no había dinero" (there was no money) to see a doctor when she sprained her knee. We also learn from Professor Rendón's poem that she is a professional woman from Laredo, Texas, who obtained her degree at the University of Michigan. Professor Rendón's identification with these social groups—ethnic, **gender,** and class—constitute her **social identities.** Again, Tajfel (1981) and others define social identity as those aspects of an individual's self-identity that derive from one's knowledge of belonging to categories and groups, together with the value and emotional significance one attaches to those memberships. Professor Rendón not only thinks of herself as a woman and a Chicana of a working-class background, but she also expresses emotional attachment and value to these group memberships. In chapter 2 "*¿Quiénes Somos?:* The Importance of Social Identity," we explore the different group memberships that define who Chicanos/as are as a people. In particular, we review the colonization history of the American Southwest, large parts of which were Mexican territory and became part of the United States at the end of the Mexican-American War in 1848. The Treaty of Guadalupe Hidalgo ceded to the United States what is now the five southwestern states of Colorado, California, New Mexico, Texas, and Arizona. Chicanos/as were born out of this act of war, and their sense of themselves as a people is influenced by this history.

Patricia Gurin and her colleagues (1980) make a distinction between two aspects of social identity:

> Identification and consciousness both denote cognitions: the former about a person's relation to others within a stratum [group], the latter about a stratum's [group's] position within a society. Identification refers to the awareness of having ideas, feelings, and interests similar to others who share the same stratum characteristics. Consciousness refers to a set of political beliefs and action orientations arising out of this awareness of similarity. (Gurin, Miller, and Gurin 1980, 143)

Identification, then, is whether individuals think of themselves as belonging to certain groups based on, say, ethnicity, gender, and class. **Consciousness** refers to whether individuals are aware that the groups they belong to hold a certain status (either powerful or not powerful) in society and whether they will take action to change this status, not just for themselves, but for other members of the group as well.

In her definition of self, Professor Rendón not only identifies with the different social groups she belongs to, but she also exhibits consciousness.

Professor Rendón acknowledges that, as a group, Mexicans are not considered as intelligent as others; that "unattractive" women are not as highly valued as women "who found their/way into school clubs and organizations/not for what they knew, but how they looked"; and that poor students cannot tell their teachers about their financial woes. That is, she is conscious of the negative judgments that others—teachers, parents, and society in general—have of the groups she belongs to at the same time that she identifies with the people that share some of her **social categories**— Mexicans, Chicanos/as, women, poor people, and Texans.

Chapter 3 "Language, Culture, and Community: Group Life in Creating and Maintaining Identities" examines the effects of group stigma on Chicana/o self-definition. Although derogated social identities have an influence at the individual level, stigma also works at a group level, where the group as a whole may be ineffectual in achieving a sense of positive well-being. In such a case, the positive reassessment of a group's culture, language, and sense of community becomes essential in individuals' positive views of self.

In chapter 4 "Conclusions: The Future of Identity Formations" we speculate how Chicana/o identities will evolve as societal conditions change. Among the conditions we examine are the demographic changes as Chicanas/os become a significant proportion of the U.S. population, as immigration from Mexico and other Latin American countries increases, as intermarriage becomes more common (especially among different **Latino/a** groups), and as the increase in educational and economic attainment influences the process of social identification.

We structured this book to increase the reader's engagement with the concepts and materials presented in each of the chapters. The glossary at the end of the book contains English translations of Spanish words used in the text, as well as specialized terms and definitions that will help the reader better understand the arguments presented in the book. At the end of each chapter is an exercise designed to be enjoyable and applied to real-life situations. The hope is that the exercises will help the reader explore the potential application of academic research to everyday life.

■ A Word about Our Perspective

Identity can be studied from many different perspectives. As social psychologists, we are interested in the **subjective definitions** individuals have about the different social groups they identify with. We are also interested in language, culture, and social context. Other psychologists, for example, developmental psychologists, may be more focused on the transitions individuals undergo from childhood to adolescence into adulthood. Clinical psychologists may be interested in the stress individuals suffer as they negotiate two different cultures or two different languages. Our purpose is different. We examine the social aspects of identity and how social context influences an individual's identification. Our analysis centers on the normative experiences of the majority of Chicanos/as rather than on individuals who may be having trouble accomplishing a healthy sense of self because of difficulties in coping. All of these perspectives are important, and exposure to them is essential to fully understanding Chicanas/os. As social psychologists, however, we examine only one slice of the process of developing a personal identity that is integrated with one's memberships in significant social groups.

Chicana/o Identity in

a Changing U.S. Society

¿Quién Soy?

The Development of Self

It is a Sunday morning in the rural town of Watsonville, California. The local economy is mostly based on agriculture, and many of the town's residents are first-generation Mexican immigrants who work in the fields and processing plants. Watsonville has one of the youngest populations in the state, with 30 percent of its population being eighteen years of age or younger. Most families are monolingual Spanish speakers with less than an elementary-school education. A group of these parents has been invited to attend Cara y Corazón (face and heart), a parenting skills workshop (see figure 1).

At eleven in the morning, fifteen parents are entering the local youth center. As they arrive, they hear *ranchero* music (Mexican country music) softly playing on a small tape deck and the smell of *pan dulce* (pastries) fills the air. They are greeted by social worker María Hurtado, who is director of a local nonprofit organization dedicated to delivering community prevention services to decrease youth violence and gang activity.

María greets each of the parents, shaking their hands, looking them straight in the eye, and smiling. She has also prepared name tags. Eventually everyone arrives and sits in a circle to start the workshop. María slowly reads the following instructions to the parents, permitting plenty of time for reflection and awareness, as the training manual states that "this exercise will trigger both negative and positive memories" (Tello 1994, 59):

Close your eyes and think back to a Sunday morning when you were a young child between five and ten years old. Where is this house? What does it smell like? What does it feel like? Is it hot, cold, warm? It's very early in the morning, and you just woke up. You open your eyes slowly and look around. What do you see? What does your room look like? Is it very dark in the room? Is anyone sleeping with you? You smell something coming from the kitchen. . . . What is it? You hear sounds. Where are they coming from? What kinds of sounds are they? How do they make you feel? You decide to get up and see what's going on. Walk throughout your house. . . . Who's cooking? Who's there? What are they doing? How do they feel on this Sunday morning?

During this exercise, many parents go into a deep reverie that makes them literally forget where they are. Many also cry as they recall times that were both painful and joyful. Among the many responses parents give to this exercise are the following:

- Many parents remembered their homes in rural Mexico, a very different setting from Watsonville.

- They remembered their mothers cooking breakfast—something aromatic like *chorizo con huevos* (sausage and eggs)—and several children sleeping in one bed to stay warm.

- There were usually only a few rooms, although most families tended to be fairly large.

- Many of their houses were rundown, with holes in the walls and windows that didn't quite work.

- Many parents remembered their parents singing along to music— usually *rancheras*—coming from small radios.

- It was during this time just before getting up and confronting the many responsibilities and hardships that these parents faced as children that they felt safe, taken care of, and loved.

This exercise is designed to help parents see the *cargas y regalos* (burdens and gifts) they received in their own background, preparing them for the next part of the workshop. In the following session, María draws a silhouette of a child's body on a large piece of butcher paper, labeling it "Alejandro." She then invites the parents to discuss the ways that their families showed *dignidad, respeto, confianza,* and *cariño* (dignity, respect, confidence, and caring) when they were growing up. These are important values to Chicano/a parents. This initiates the discussion of the regalos that parents have to offer their children and that are a continuation of their own upbringing. As parents give examples, the facilitator writes on a card one key word summarizing the regalo, which a parent tapes on Alejandro's silhouette, symbolizing the regalos he is receiving by such treatment. María then asks the parents to reflect on the effects these regalos might have on a

■ 1. María Hurtado conducting a Cara y Corazón workshop

child's identity. Parents quickly surmise that the more regalos a child receives, the more likely the child is to feel happy, secure, joyful, and confident and to develop self-worth.

Next, María asks the parents to discuss the cargas they experienced growing up—be it alcoholism in the family or parents never showing affection, yelling at them, belittling them, or even abusing them. As each parent discusses such an experience, he or she takes one of the cards from Alejandro's silhouette and tears it up. At the end, Alejandro has very few, if any, regalos left. Parents are then asked to think about how they may be giving their children the cargas they inherited from their own childhood and how they can replace these with regalos. For each example they give of replacing cargas with regalos, they again write a few words on a card and tape it back on Alejandro's silhouette. At the end, María asks the parents to reflect on how replacing cargas with regalos might affect Alejandro's identity development.

This description illustrates a few of the exercises parents go through as they connect their own background and their **socialization practices** to their child's development of a positive sense of self. Jerry Tello, the creator of the Cara y Corazón workshop, explicitly states that all children, in addition to having their basic physical needs met (such as shelter and food), also need nurturance, love, and stability to develop a healthy sense of self. However, as the excerpt from a Cara y Corazón workshop illustrates, these essentials are provided in culturally specific ways. Mr. Tello's assumptions run counter to the **assimilation** framework, in which Chicano/a parents are urged to adopt mainstream, middle-class (mostly white) socialization values. Instead, Mr. Tello urges facilitators like María Hurtado to respect parents' cultural and linguistic backgrounds, and to assume that all families provide their members with both regalos and cargas. The development of a positive sense of self in children is achieved by fostering parents' regalos while making them conscious of their cargas so they can modify their parenting behaviors.

In this chapter we examine the regalos the social psychological literature tells us are necessary for children to develop a positive sense of self. As the Cara y Corazón workshop indicates, we recognize that parenting is affected by "societal, cultural, familial, and individual elements" (Tello 1994, 61). Like all children, Chicana/o children thrive when they are given love, affirmation, and reassurance, and when their basic physical needs are met. Yet, Chicano/a children have additional cargas they must deal with that children from the dominant culture do not bear. Among these are the development of a positive sense of self that encompasses their ethnicity, race, class, and **gender.**

■ The Development of a Positive Sense of Self: Ethnicity, Race, Class, and Gender

What happens "when peoples meet," as the phrase goes? Such meetings in the modern world are likely to take place under a variety of circumstances: colonial conquest, military conquest, military occupation, redrawing of national boundaries to include diverse ethnic groups, large-scale trade and missionary activity, technical assistance to underdeveloped countries, displacement of an aboriginal population, and voluntary immigration which increases the ethnic diversity of a host country. In the American continental experience, the last two types have been the decisive ones. (Gordon 1964, 60)

Gordon (1964, 60) reminds us that "sociologists and cultural anthropologists have described the processes and results of ethnic 'meetings' under such terms as 'assimilation' and '**acculturation,**'" terms that many times have been used interchangeably. The study of Chicanos/as in the United States has been studied predominantly from an **assimilation**/acculturation framework.

The 1960s: Assimilation

In the 1960s, the goal in ethnic identity research was to discover the best way to accelerate assimilation. The prevailing view was that, like the early waves of European immigrants at the turn of the nineteenth century, everybody should strive to be "American," forget their native language and culture, and become part of the great American melting pot. Schools were essential in implementing what was called a policy of "Americanization" (Garcia and Hurtado 1995). This was not necessarily a malicious position; rather it was offered as the solution to Chicanos/as becoming part of the middle class and bettering their lives.

The assimilation policy, however, had a very high psychological cost for Chicano/a children (see topic highlight 1). Most children feel uncomfortable over being singled out as different and prefer to fit in with their peers. However, many Chicanos/as during this time, as is true today, started school speaking Spanish and had parents who were not familiar with the culture and values of the schools their children were attending.

As part of this Americanization policy, many schools in the Southwest, especially in states like Texas, New Mexico, and Arizona, had rules against speaking Spanish on school grounds. Students reported having been spanked, given detention, fined a quarter, made to run laps, and even having their mouths taped shut for violating the policy (Hurtado and Rodríguez 1989). Many Chicano/a parents during this historical period found it difficult to give their children a healthy sense of self when there was such a disjuncture between the schools' position on cultural diversity and many parents' desire to retain their language and their culture. Some parents, fearing their children would not succeed in school, chose not to teach their children Spanish—a decision that many of these children later resented when as adults they could not communicate with relatives and others in their communities.

During the 1960s much of the research on ethnic identity was focused on measuring levels of assimilation. Assimilation was generally defined as "a process of interpenetration and fusion in which persons and groups acquire the memories, sentiments, and attitudes of other persons or groups, and, by sharing their experience and history, are incorporated with them in

Topic Highlight 1. Assimilation: My Early Years

Adapted from Aída Hurtado (1997)

In this highlight I combine my own personal experiences of how my identi-fications as a Chicana and as a woman have evolved over the years and how my own quandaries about multiple group identifications echo with the research on assimilation/acculturation over the last forty-four years.

I started first grade in Toledo, Ohio, in the early 1960s because my parents were part of the migrant stream that headed to the northern United States from south Texas to pick crops during the summer months. Like many labor migrants, we eventually settled in the Midwest, and I attended an elementary school experiencing "white flight" as African Americans moved into the neighborhood. There was only one other Mexican family living in the area. At the time, we were supposed to try to fit in and be like the European immigrants before us, striving to be "Americans," forgetting our language and culture, and becoming part of the great American melting pot. In exchange for assimilating, we were promised the "American Dream."

This expectation was particularly strong for students like me who learned English quickly without the aid of bilingual education and who did very well in school. The emotional cost to me, however, was very high. Like most kids, I hated being different in any way. I pretended I didn't speak Spanish, and I wanted my mom to wear pearls like June Cleaver in the television show "Leave It to Beaver." I always felt uneasy in school despite my success, and certainly it was not a place where my parents, or their history and culture, were welcomed. My emerging multiplicity of identities resulting from my many significant group memberships was not recognized in school. There was no one to help me understand the many cultural and class dislocations I was experiencing as a dark-skinned, working-class, Mexican, and Spanish-speaking daughter of immigrant parents. ■

a common cultural life" (Park and Burgess 1921, 735). Many of the assimilation scales developed during this time were designed to measure the quickest and most efficient way to assimilate immigrants. The assimilation framework did not examine gender and was uncritically applied to all groups regardless of race, history in the United States, forms of incorporation in the United States, or reasons for immigrating.

The 1970s: Acculturation

By the 1970s research on ethnic identity had changed emphasis. When Milton Gordon published his influential book, *Assimilation in American Life,* in 1964, he made the important conceptual distinction between assimilation and **acculturation** and highlighted the fact that there could be different dimensions to both of these social processes. According to Gordon,

(1) cultural assimilation, or acculturation, is likely to be the first of the types of assimilation to occur when a minority group arrives on the scene; and (2) cultural assimilation, or acculturation, of the minority group may take place even when none of the other types of assimilation [structural, marital, identificational, attitude receptional, behavior receptional, and civic] occurs simultaneously or later, and this condition of "acculturation only" may continue indefinitely. (Gordon 1964, 77)

Gordon's important conceptual distinction between assimilation and acculturation cemented the *trait approach* to the study of cultural diversity (Hurtado 1997). In this approach, the goal of empirical work is to find those traits each group has in common with the dominant white group. The minority group is judged more or less acculturated/assimilated to the dominant group depending on the number of traits the two groups have in common (see figure 2). For example, African Americans have language and citizenship in common with whites, while Asians have educational and achievement values in common with whites, and Chicanos/as may have race in common with whites. The trait approach allows for variations in levels of acculturation and levels of assimilation among individuals and groups. Gordon's greatest contribution was the notion that even if an individual is highly acculturated (or culturally assimilated)—for example, speaks English, graduates from college, and is socially skilled in the dominant culture—he or she can still remain unassimilated on other dimensions. For example, the individual may live in a predominantly ethnic neighborhood, marry a member of her or his own group, and belong

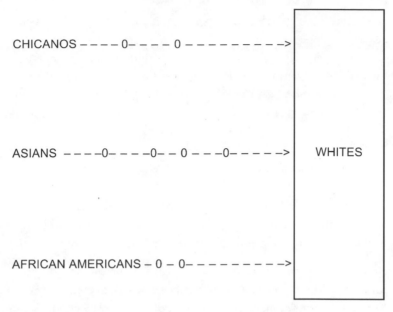

CHICANOS – – – – 0– – – – 0 – – – – – – – – –>

ASIANS – – – –0– – – –0– – 0 – – –0– – – – –>   WHITES

AFRICAN AMERICANS – 0 – 0– – – – – – – – –>

■ 2. Assimilation model: the trait approach to the study of cultural and social differences

mostly to civic organizations within her or his own community. Although this paradigm may seem commonsensical in current thinking about ethnicity, it was revolutionary at the time because it allowed for nuances of cultural adaptation, for empirical measurement of these different dimensions, and for different levels and combinations of acculturation and assimilation. Most importantly, it allowed for structurally assimilated individuals, as measured by income and education, to retain their ethnic **identification** with and loyalty to their communities of origin.

The trait approach to the study of cultural differences, however, ignores contextual factors, gender, ethnicity, and racial diversity within groups. For example, the historical period in which individuals grow up also makes an enormous difference on how they negotiate acculturation (see topic highlight 2).

By the 1970s ethnicity was no longer something to hide or be ashamed of. This was the height of the **Chicano Movement,** which advocated a nativist return beyond Mexican culture to Chicanos'/as' Aztec roots, which became iconic of Chicano/a identity. Similarly, much of the research on ethnic groups was experiencing a revolution of sorts. Instead of assimilation being the solution to ethnic diversity, the concept of acculturation

Topic Highlight 2. My Young Adulthood: Acculturation

Adapted from Aída Hurtado (1997)

I started first grade in the Midwest as the only Mexican, Spanish-speaking girl in my class, and the issue of acculturation was something that I had to negotiate the first time I entered a classroom. Furthermore, I had to negotiate it differently than the boys in the same context did. By the time I was in high school, my family had moved back to south Texas—a geographical area where Spanish was spoken almost universally. The question of my ethnicity and language were posed very differently than if we had remained in the Midwest, where I was in the minority dealing with these issues.

By the time I graduated from high school in 1972, and certainly by the time I graduated from college in 1975, the way I thought about my identities had changed. The historical times deeply influenced my views on my ethnicity. By the time I was in college, my ethnic background was not something to hide or be ashamed of, but something to be embraced. This was the height of the Chicano Movement, and we reclaimed our Mexican culture and had a hunger for our Aztec origins, which we actually knew very little about. Nonetheless, our Indian roots became icons of our Chicano identity. This was the era when many Chicano activists named their children unpronounceable Aztec names such as Tizoc, Xochitl, and Saguache. ■

reached its height of popularity. In fact, the prevalent view was that minorities could become culturally and linguistically acculturated to the mainstream without becoming completely assimilated, and that being bicultural was a viable option. This is not to imply, however, that the assimilation framework disappeared, but rather it became a bit more refined and, at times, coexisted with the beliefs about acculturation.

Gender as a category of analysis was absent in this paradigm, even though the white feminist movement was at its height during this period. Many Chicanas and other women of Color embraced aspects of the femi-

nist movement to understand their role as women, but their concerns were
never fully integrated into their respective ethnic and racial movements,
nor were feminists' concerns integrated into our understanding of ethnic
identity in much of the scholarship of the time.

The 1980s: The Internal Colonial Model

By the 1980s, researchers had begun integrating many of the analyses
developed through ethnic studies. Chicanos/as were no longer thought of
as another "immigrant group" just like European immigrants. Instead,
their history of colonization was recognized as an integral part of the
development of their ethnic identity. Chicana/o scholars proposed that the
experience of conquest that began in 1848 was somewhat similar to what
Native Americans had experienced with the taking of their lands (see topic
highlight 3). Furthermore, although Chicanos/as were not as racially distinct from European Americans as were African Americans, their mixed

heritage of Spanish, Indian, and African blood made them **mestizos** subject to race discrimination, regardless of how they were classified in the U.S. census (i.e., as white). This approach was known as the **internal colonial model** (Almaguer, 1974; Blauner, 1972).

From this perspective, the problems encountered by ethnic and racial minorities as they adapted to the majority culture were not the result of "culture conflict" generated by differences in traits between dominant and subordinate groups, as the assimilation/acculturation framework would have us believe. Rather, the internal colonial model proposed that the cultural adaptations of ethnic and racial groups were the outcome of "the organization of the economic structure of U.S. capitalism and from the labor relationships that generate that particular mode of production" (Almaguer 1974, 43). This analysis had substantial empirical and theoretical support from what Baca Zinn (1995) calls the revisionist scholarship that prevailed in ethnic studies during the late 1970s and into the early part of the 1980s (Baca Zinn 1995; Hurtado 1995; Zavella 1987).

By the 1980s, ethnic identification had grown more complex, especially in states where there were many different cultural groups and where intergroup contact had increased significantly from previous decades. Chief among these was the state of California. However, gender still was not analyzed in this paradigm.

1990s to the Present: The Social Engagement Model

The **social engagement model** (Hurtado 1997) is an alternative to the assimilation/acculturation framework for understanding cultural transformations. The social engagement model examines groups' spheres of social involvement. The concept of sphere is similar to what social psychologist Kurt Lewin (1948) called a life space, which he defined as the total subjective environment each person experiences (see figure 3).

A life space can be as small as a classroom or a school and as large as a country or a continent. Although the principles of the social engagement model can be applied to any social spheres defined by a researcher, in this book we focus on four spheres: work, family, school, and community (see figure 4). According to Lewin, the role of the social psychologist is to understand how an individual defines from his or her subjective point of view a particular life space to better understand that individual's motivations and behaviors.

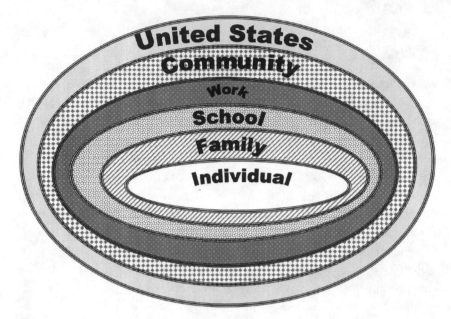

■ 3. An individual's possible life spaces according to Kurt Lewin, highlighting the importance of one's environment over one's personal characteristics in determining identity

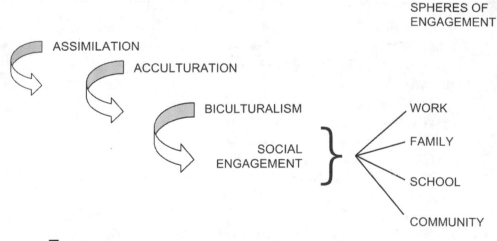

■ 4. Theoretical developments in the study of ethnic identity, leading to the social engagement model

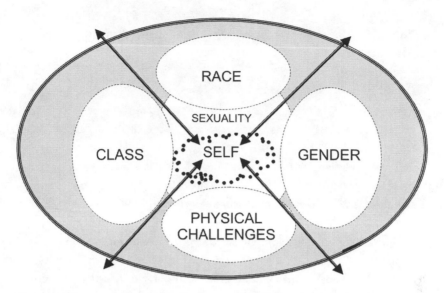

■ 5. An individual's life space: the creation of self through intersectionality

The social engagement model follows Kurt Lewin's theoretical emphasis on examining an individual's engagement in the life spaces he or she subjectively defines. This is called a *definitional approach*, because instead of researchers relying solely on their definition of social engagement, the individual's subjective definitions are what guides the research. The researcher systematically asks participants in a social sphere (for example, parents whose children attend a particular school) to define what they mean by engagement (say, participation in their children's schools). Furthermore, the model recognizes that participation in any sphere of social engagement may be either facilitated or hampered by the individuals' significant **social identities** based on gender, class, ethnicity, race, sexuality, physical challenges, and other factors (see figure 5). For example, parents who are poor Mexican immigrants with very little formal education will have a very different engagement with their children's school than will parents who are white, English-speaking, middle-class professionals.

The significance and relationship between these different social identities (e.g., class, race, ethnicity, sexuality) vary from social sphere to social sphere and across time. In some circumstances, one particular group membership or set of memberships may be more important than others. In other circumstances, for example, when functioning within a group that is homogenous with regard to their significant group social identities, a particular social identity (or identities) may be much less relevant than in a situation where many groups interact with each other (see topic highlight 4). For example, a university student may not think about being Mexican when interacting with family members, but will do so when answering a question in a classroom where he or she is the only person of Mexican descent. In addition, a person may define a particular group membership differently at one time than at another. For example, a young person growing up in a predominantly Chicano/a neighborhood may take his or her ethnicity for granted. Attending a university and taking courses on Chicano history and culture may provide the impetus for this person to reassess ethnicity and its salience and importance.

Let us provide a concrete example of research that illustrates the difference between using an assimilation/acculturation framework and the social engagement model. Research findings indicate that Chicano/a parents do not participate in their children's schools as much as white parents do. School participation is usually defined in terms of

- attending parent-teacher association (PTA) meetings,
- attending parent-teacher conferences,
- attending back-to-school nights,
- participating in their children's classrooms, and
- attending individual parent-teacher and parent-principal meetings.

This definition of school participation is from the dominant group's perspective, not from Chicano/a parents' view of what is possible or desirable for them. In our study of Chicano/a and white parents in an elementary magnet school in a rural northern California town, we applied the social engagement model to school participation (Hurtado 1994), to answer the following research questions:

- Were there different groups of parents in the school's life space?
- If so, how do different groups of parents *subjectively* define their participation?
- Do different groups of parents define the barriers to their participation differently?

The answer to the first research question indicated three groups of parents:

- U.S.–born, English-speaking, working-class Chicano/a parents,
- Mexican-born, Spanish-speaking immigrant parents, mostly farmworkers, and
- U.S.–born, English-speaking, white professional parents.

The white parents indeed participated in the school through the usual avenues described earlier. Chicano/a parents, however, had much more variation in their participation. Although the Chicano/a parents in general participated in their children's schools through ethnically based activities like a Mexican folk dance troupe and a school mariachi band, the English-speaking Chicano/a parents were more likely to talk to teachers than the Spanish-speaking immigrant parents were.

The social engagement model—which has at its core a definitional approach to differences in school participation—sheds a different light on the results of the study. First of all, besides the standard measures of school participation, there were measures that allowed different groups of parents to provide their own definitions of what they considered school participation and why. Taking this perspective in our study, we found that most Chicano/a parents, regardless of generation in the United States, viewed cultural activities held at school facilities after hours as a very important part of their connection to the school. These cultural activities included a weekly Mexican folkloric dancing class and a weekly Mexican folkloric music class. The parents had also organized a performance group, which gave students opportunities to display their talents in various community events. The activities were largely organized by the parents themselves and were funded through bake sales and donations. Moreover, these activities were conducted at great costs to the Chicano/a parents, since most of them worked very long hours at minimum or below minimum wage.

Chicano/a parents indicated the following factors as barriers to traditional school participation:

- language barriers for Spanish-speaking parents,
- conflicts between work schedules and school activities (the English-speaking Chicano/a parents being mostly single parents, and the Spanish-speaking Chicano/a parents mostly farmworkers who worked very long hours), and
- intimidation because they were unfamiliar with school etiquette.

Most of the immigrant parents spoke only Spanish, whereas most of the teachers spoke only English. Even the teachers who spoke Spanish were mostly white, which intimidated most of the immigrant parents. Furthermore, most of the immigrant and Chicano/a English-speaking parents worked very long hours, mostly in unskilled and semiskilled jobs, which prevented them from attending back-to-school nights and some of the parent-teacher conferences. School officials never considered scheduling these events according to Chicano/a parents' particular work demands. The school's status as a magnet elementary school attracted white students from an affluent suburb some distance from the school. The white families either had mothers who stayed at home or professional parents with flexibility to rearrange their work schedules to attend school functions.

Lastly, the immigrant parents who had tried to approach teachers reported that they felt rebuffed because they did not understand the etiquette for approaching white professionals. The English-speaking Chicano/a parents did not feel as much distance from teachers as the immigrant parents did, and neither did the white parents. Teachers were very surprised to see the differences in the parents' reports of the number of times they spoke to teachers. The teachers felt they had had equal amounts of contact with all parents regardless of ethnicity, race, and language background. Teachers were even more surprised to find out that out of 609 students, there were only 120 white students, the rest were almost entirely Chicano/a (with a few Asian American and a few African American students). As a group, the white parents had such a strong presence in the elementary school that many teachers thought the student composition was more evenly distributed among the different ethnic and racial groups.

No such barriers were expressed by any of the white parents. However, they too felt changes would improve their participation in the school. First, many of the white mothers volunteered in the school and spent a great deal of time on the premises. They suggested a lounge where they could spend time and connect with other parents to facilitate their participation.

Following the assimilation/acculturation framework, which measures only the conventional indicators of school participation, the results could be summarized as: Immigrant parents do not participate in their children's schools, which leads to higher levels of academic failure. Second-generation and beyond Chicano/a parents become more acculturated by learning English and therefore begin to participate in their children's school with similar behaviors to those of their white counterparts. White parents participate far more in their children's school in ways that lead to higher educational achievement. Accordingly, we need to urge immigrant parents to assimilate/acculturate as quickly as possible to increase their children's educational achievement.

The assimilation/acculturation framework assumes that all groups of parents have an equal opportunity to participate in their children's school. The school and the staff are not examined, and particular measures of school participation are assumed to be appropriate for all groups of parents. Furthermore, because white parents score the highest on traditional scales of school participation, they are inadvertently set up as the model that Chicano/a parents should emulate, reinforcing the trait-approach to the study of cultural differences (see figure 2). Possible approaches to increase parent participation and student achievement suggested from the assimilation/acculturation framework are:

- Make all students more like middle-class white students.
- Do not recognize diversity within the white or Chicano/a populations or design interventions to address this diversity.
- If interventions fail, create different schools, increasing segregation.

Using an assimilation/acculturation framework does not permit Chicano/a parents to contribute their own perceptions and definitions of what constitutes school participation nor for those definitions to influence the definitions of white parents. The internal variation within each group of parents is not explored to gain insights about varying definitions of school participation. Most importantly, although white students had, on average, higher academic achievement than Chicano/a students did, there were a substantial number of immigrant children and second-generation Chicano/a children who performed well in school. There were also white students who performed as poorly as Chicano/a students. By focusing on *average differences* between groups, the assimilation/acculturation framework fails to examine areas of similarity, and by ignoring gender, it also fails to identify that girls, on average, do better academically than boys, regardless of ethnicity or race.

The social engagement model permits the study of similarities and differences. The different groups of parents had important differences. Among these were:

- social class,
- culture,
- language,
- family composition,
- number of two-parent households, and
- number of single-parent households.

However, there were also important similarities, especially when parents were asked what kind of students they wanted the schools to produce. Almost all parents wanted students to be able to

- read and write,
- follow rules,
- be timely on their assignments,
- be held accountable to just rules,
- develop critical judgments when students are confronted with difficult situations.

That is, parents, regardless of their different *social identities,* were in agreement about what kind of **personal identities** they wanted their children to develop within the school setting. Again, an assimilation/acculturation framework does not allow for the examination of similarities from which these three very different sets of parents can work to enhance their children's education.

These results were presented in a meeting with the teachers, school staff, school administrators, and parent representatives. These differences and similarities generated a lively and cooperative discussion, which was simultaneously translated for the Spanish-speaking parent representatives.

One of the findings concerning household composition that most surprised the participants in this meeting was that immigrant households and white households had mostly two-parent families, whereas non-immigrant Chicano/a households were mostly composed of single mothers. The Chicana single mothers felt particularly stressed because they lacked support to involve their children in school activities, including the cultural ones. Parent representatives suggested organizing a group to address this need. Some white parent representatives were intrigued with the after-school cultural activities and inquired about whether their children could participate in these events. The other finding that surprised all participants in the meeting was that almost all school participation, regardless of how it was defined, was done by women. Fathers, regardless of ethnicity, race, or immigrant status, rarely participated in school activities. Furthermore, almost all socialization tasks at home that we asked about—such as making children do their homework, keeping a regular bedtime schedule, and taking responsibility for ensuring consistent school attendance—were defined as women's responsibilities in most families, including the ones where women worked outside the home for very long hours. This finding generated a great deal of discussion and concern about fathers' lack of school participation and socialization responsibilities. At the same time, it also generated strategies for increasing the participation of *all* fathers in future school events. Below is a list of interventions that resulted from this process, in which all parents felt included:

- Take into account parents' work schedules.
- Expand hours for parent events and provide flexibility in scheduling.
- Provide English-Spanish translators for school activities.
- Diversify school activities to include **Latino/a** cultural practices.
- Provide a lounge for parent volunteers at the school.
- Encourage the participation of white students in Latino/a cultural activities, and encourage Latino/a students to participate in all school activities.
- Increase outreach to all fathers to encourage their participation in school activities.

This is not necessarily a story with a happy ending, but it is a story that has begun to seriously address multiple group identifications and how these differentially affect individuals' behaviors. The social engagement model recognizes that there are many ways to participate in school activities that benefit children. No one type of school participation is set up as the ideal, with deviation from it considered deficient. Instead, the researcher's task is to carefully document the life space under study with complete attention to all different groups involved, and to design interventions that take this diversity into account. What is most important is that the story that the social engagement model produces is decidedly different from the one that emerges from an assimilation/acculturation framework.

■ Conclusions: Multiple Social Adaptations to Cultural Transformations

The increasing number of Chicanos/as and other Latinos/as in the United States, most of whom are immigrants, has implications for their cultural adaptations and their social and ethnic identification. These changes also influence how willing ethnic and racial groups are to relinquish their ethnic distinctiveness (see topic highlight 5).

Unlike the turn of the last century, when the dominant ideology was to

Topic Highlight 5. Future Identity Formations

Adapted from Aída Hurtado (1997)

After nineteen years at the University of California, Santa Cruz, I have seen five generations of college students graduate. Many of these students have even finished graduate school or law school, have married, and are raising children. I believe the cultural and social adaptations of these students illustrate what academics and professionals will have to address in their work and communities. Tizoc, a fourth-generation Californian, married a first-generation immigrant Mexicana, Lizbeth. They have a child whom they named Anastacia in honor of Lizbeth's great-great-grandmother, who was a *soldadera* (female soldier) in the Mexican Revolution. Saguache married a Salvadoran immigrant, Yvette, and they have a child named Sandino, in honor of the Nicaraguan revolutionary. They travel often to El Salvador because they want their child to grow up with knowledge of his mother's native country. Xochitl married an Irish American, and they speak only Spanish in their home because they want their little boy to be bilingual. They named him Carlos Murphy. Obviously, there is much work to be done to fully understand future ethnic identity formations. ■

make all ethnic groups into non—ethnically distinct Americans, in the twenty-first century ethnic and racial groups do not necessarily perceive their ethnicity as a barrier to their social and economic integration (Hurtado, Rodríguez, Gurin, and Beals 1993). The current social and historical context in the United States favors multiculturalism. Although the concept of multiculturalism is contested, the fact remains that there is a vibrant debate that encourages at least some ethnic group members (with some white group members agreeing) that ethnic cultural maintenance should not be a detriment to economic and social advancement (Phinney 1996).

Furthermore, the debates around multiculturalism have problematized the notion of free choice in cultural adaptations that is inherent in the concepts of acculturation and assimilation. All assimilation/acculturation theorists discuss the role of prejudice and discrimination, but these two processes are analyzed separately rather than as integral parts of the negotiation around cultural adaptations (Gurin, Hurtado, and Peng 1994). In other words, the concepts of assimilation and acculturation do not take into account how power differentials in society affect cultural adaptations. Also absent is the consideration of racial differences between ethnic groups and the dominant society and how they affect cultural adaptations. Rarely is ethnic identity theoretically or empirically tied to class, race, gender, and sexual identification, or to any other significant group memberships (Hurtado, Rodríguez, Gurin, and Beals 1993). Most importantly, the study of gender has been segregated from the study of ethnicity, especially for Chicanos/as and Latinos/as.

■ Summary

Given all these complexities, Chicano/a parents have a difficult task littered with many obstacles in creating a sense of security, confidence, and self-worth in their children. Interventions like Cara y Corazón help parents, especially those who have not had the opportunity for formal education, to reflect and construct tools to overcome these hurdles.

- Parents affect their children through regalos—such as dignity, respect, confidence, love, and affection—and through cargas, such as belittling children in various ways. It is the regalos that are crucial for creating a positive personal identity.

- Americanization pressures, as expressed in the assimilation and acculturation frameworks, led researchers to overlook the importance of the unique history of colonization for persons of Mexican descent living in the United States. The internal colonial model was an influential corrective to the omissions of the assimilation and acculturation frameworks.

- The social engagement model further redresses those omissions by taking the important step of asking people themselves how they define engagement and how they want to participate in the social spheres of work, family, school, and community.

In this chapter we provided an example of how the social engagement model helps us understand the ways Chicano/a English-speaking parents, Mexican immigrant Spanish-speaking parents, and white English-speaking parents define (a) participation in their children's schools, (b) how they want to participate, (c) the barriers they see to participating as they would like, and (d) how these three groups of parents are both different from and similar to each other. An assimilation/acculturation model would not reveal this rich picture of engagement in schools.

In the next chapter we will explore another aspect of an individual's self-conception: social identity. Social identity refers to that aspect of self that is composed of the individual's group memberships and the emotional value he or she attaches to them.

■ Discussion Exercises

A Day with Alejandro

Alejandro is five years old.

It's early Friday morning, and Alejandro is sound asleep. His mother comes to wake him.

"Alejandro, Wake up! It's time to get ready for school! You know it's a school day. Why can't you wake yourself up? I already have to wake your dad up, take care of the baby, and I don't have time to take care of you! Now hurry up and get up." She leaves the room.

As Alejandro wipes his eyes and starts to sit up, his mother comes back in.

"Alejandro hurry up! Why are you moving so slowly? You know that I have to hurry up. If you're late for school you'll have no one to blame but yourself."

"But, Mom, I'm tired; the baby kept crying and I couldn't sleep, and I was getting . . ."

"I don't have time for you to be tired, you've got to get up and go to school. Put these clothes on."

"I don't want to wear that orange and blue shirt! The kids at school say I look dumb."

"Don't be silly, the kids are just playing with you. Now get dressed and go eat breakfast."

When Alejandro gets to the breakfast table, his father and sister are eating.

"Good morning, Papá! Good morning, 'manita [little sister]!"

"There's no time for talking. You better hurry up and eat, young man. I don't want to be late."

"But, I just sat down and Mami said . . ."

"Don't talk back to me! If you're not going to respect me, I'll get the belt out. I don't want to hear any problems about you in school. Do you hear?"

"Sí, Papá."

The previous text is a description taken from one of the exercises in the Cara y Corazón workshop manual. Do the following with a small group of students:

1. Read the story out loud.

2. Write on separate note cards the cargas and the regalos you can identify in Alejandro's story.

3. Make two separate piles, one for regalos and one for cargas.

4. Review the stack of regalos first, by reading each note card out loud and discussing how that regalo might affect Alejandro's identity as he grows up. Relate it to your own upbringing and reflect on how it affected you as a person.

5. Review the stack of cargas in the same way.

6. Now, take the stack of cargas and try to turn them into regalos. How can a parent say the same thing to a young child (for example, to get dressed in the morning), but in a way that makes the child feel loved and affirmed rather than diminished? Try to relate as many of these issues as you can to your own upbringing and how your sense of identity was affected by them.

¿Quiénes Somos?

The Importance of Social Identity

The essay below was written by an undergraduate as part of an exercise in one of our classes to build a **social identity** altar (see figure 6).

My Altar

The project was to present an altar of myself. *Myself.* This word rang hard in my soul because the myself isn't an easy presentation. The myself are multiple identities screaming at the top of their lungs to be heard that they are being crushed by each other and that space is needed to breathe. The myself is a collaboration of sweat, tears, blood, and exhaustion. The myself is the idea that my different identities want to be heard, but the more they are expressed, the more they feel erased throughout the utter confusion of the whole ordeal of wanting to be recognized. My goal for this project was to not reject myself. To not hide myself. And the first thing I looked for was the first thing I was not supposed to do. I looked at other people. Now the logic behind this makes sense. How do we find out about ourselves if we don't look at the environment that we are in? So as the first statement about my altar I put no pictures up, to represent that it was about me that the altar was for. Because, all my life I was taught only to think of others, give to others, sacrifice myself for others, where my existence began to deteriorate into hating myself. I feel the biggest accomplishment I've had in my life was not in being considerate of others, but in being considerate of myself. To love myself proved to be the hardest task when no one acknowledged me, they only acknowledged my services and what I was capable of. Objectifying me, rippling myself into believing as much.

The main parts of my altar are a mirror, flowers, and food. I mean, there are other parts that represent my family, girlfriends, even the books,

■ 6. Social identity altar built in Chicana feminisms class by Dr. Sandra Pacheco, October 2002

which were what I chose to have as a base of my identity. And even though every aspect is important on that altar, I want to share what I feel are the main parts. (Marisol Lorenzana 2001)

The class exercise described above is based on a tradition practiced in Mexico and the rest of Latin America of building altars to celebrate **El Día de los Muertos.** This holiday takes place in the fall and has been appropri-

■ 7. Amalia Mesa-Bains's altar to Mexican actress Dolores del Río

ated by Chicano/a communities, especially Chicano/a artists, to highlight social justice issues (among other things) in their communities (see figure 7). Lourdes Portillo's film, *La Ofrenda* (The Offering) traces the practice from rural areas in Mexico to the Mission District in San Francisco, California, a predominantly **Latino/a** neighborhood.

The essay at the beginning of this chapter underscores many of the characteristics of social identities as delineated by social psychologists. In the rest of this chapter, we discuss how the distinction between personal and social identity helps us understand how individuals develop their sense of self.

Personal Identity and Social Identity

Myself. This word rang hard in my soul because the *myself* isn't an easy presentation. The *myself* are multiple identities screaming at the top of their lungs to be heard that they are being crushed by each other and that space is needed to breathe. (Marisol Lorenzana 2001)

In the introduction, we made a general distinction between **personal identity** and **social identity.** In the last chapter we examined personal identity, which Henri Tajfel (1981) and others define as an aspect of the self composed of psychological traits and dispositions that give us personal uniqueness. Personal identity is derived from intrapsychic influences, many of which are socialized within families. From this perspective, human beings have a great deal in common precisely because our personal identities entail such universal activities as loving, mating, raising children, and doing productive work. These activities are universal components of how individuals define who they are. Personal identity is much more stable and coherent over time than is social identity. Most individuals do not have multiple personal identities, nor do their personal identities change markedly from social context to social context (Hurtado 1996).

Following Tajfel (1981), social identity is different from personal identity. Social identity is defined as the aspects of an individual's self-identity that derive from his or her knowledge of being a member of categories and groups, together with the value and emotional significance attached to those memberships (Tajfel 1978, 63). When Lorenzana writes "the myself" as "multiple identities," she is describing her *social identities* not her *personal identity.* In fact, from reading Lorenzana's narrative, we get a strong sense of who she is as a person.

Below we examine two poems that illuminate the difference between personal identity and social identity. In the poem "Disco Gymnasium," Chicana writer Michelle Serros (1993, 15–16) portrays a young woman who has difficulty going to the gym because she would rather eat a chimichanga than exercise:

Disco Gymnasium

The eighteen inch waist
    buxom blonde
informs me,
    "You're late!
    Bathrooms are a mess!"
I tell her,
    "No, I'm no cleaning lady
    I go here, I'm a member."
Her left eyebrow arches
with suspicion
she checks my plastic card
    proof and signature,
        annoyed wave,
        allows me in.
Feeling very intrusive
In this exclusive
gym,
no bobby socks
or baggy shorts
like Rio de Valle Jr. High
P.E. Class,
I'm the solo *mexicana*
in loose *chongo*
ex-boyfriend's sweatpants
oversize T-shirt

fashion outcast
creating a nuisance
to iridescent,
    pearlescent,
        adolescents!
spandex,
    latex,
        triple X!
    Ahead and behind
    my eyes can't hide from
    the neon green thong thang

dividing large curd
twin cheeks.

It's the Friday afternoon
last ditch effort
to get it on
and get it off
with wealthy white westside women
sweating to inner city rap boys
      (like they secretly do at home).
Kick,
    higher!
Stretch
    longer!
Squeeze
    tighter
DIE
    sooner!

And the whole time
I am thinking of
that double cheese
chimichanga supreme
I'm gonna pick up
on the way home.

In another poem Serros (1993, 17–20) describes a middle-aged secretary who dresses as a *'chuca* and commands respect through her demeanor:

What Is Bad

Donna Rodriguez is bad.
More than bad
she has the power
the kind of power
that gets respect
the kind of respect
I envy.

Every Monday morning
like a movie star

encased by tinted windows
her black Trans-Am
pulls up into employee lot
takes up two spaces,
nobody dare complain.

Now that is BAD.

All the employees,
men, women alike
part the way
heads humbly bow
so Donna can make her way
to the company time clock.
Suit of armor she wears well
fifty lbs. extra flesh
padding a forty-eight double-D brassiere
sweat rings saturating size 29 blouse.
She slowly strolls by,
petite crucifix sways on a chain
sharing space with a gold plated
self proclamation:
100% BITCH
diamond chip
dotting the "i."

Now that is BAD.

At lunch break
the Anglo women shudder in fear
as Donna whips out Weight Watchers Mexi-cuisine.
She's on a diet (again).
It's gonna be a long week.
They pretend to be her friend
get on her good side early
ask about Hector,
her 19 year old baby behind bars,
the red press on nails,
and does she have a good recipe for salsa?

Donna knows their game.
Stays silent
takes long slow drags
off Marlboro Lites
her eyes squint
judging their sloppy eyeliner
creaseless corduroys
tofu tacos.

After letting out a post battle yawn
she heads back to her cubicles
plural,
while all us are crammed
into pet size squares,
Donna gets two
all for herself,
"I'm a big woman.
I need bigger space."
And she gets it,
just like that.

Now that is BAD.

The boss is terrified of her.
It's rumored
he recently saw *Zootsuit* on Showtime
and with her white eye shadow
penciled in brows
baby tattoo
nestled between thumb and finger
he suspects she could have
been
might very well still be
a *'chuca,*
as in *pachuca,*
a nonexistent breed
in his Westside life
but here she is

now
living large in the workplace
his workplace,
and he doesn't want any trouble.
Mr. Equal Opportunity Employer,
and scared.

Scared of Donna
who gets weekends off
extended lunches
advance loans
leaves work early on Fridays
to make it to bank,
writes in own hours
on time card.

Now that is *bad*.
That's respect.
And I want it.

Even though Donna and the narrator in "Disco Gymnasium" have four important social identities in common—**gender,** ethnicity, class, and race—they are very different individuals. When one of us asked students in our class to describe the two women in the poem, they came up with the list of personal characteristics displayed in figure 8. The similarity in these two women's social identities does not preclude them from being unique individuals who can be powerful, intimidating, and savvy, as students described Donna, or strong, funny, and observant, as students described the narrator in "Disco Gymnasium."

The four social identities these two women have in common—ethnicity, gender, social class, and race—are so powerful that most people would attribute immense similarity to all individuals who share them. Working-class women of Mexican descent are perceived as being more similar than different, and indeed the women in both poems would agree they have some similarities because of their social identities. Among these are

- country of origin,
- language background,

Los Angeles Life Space

SOCIAL IDENTITIES IN COMMON

Gender, Ethnicity, Class, Race

DIFFERENCES IN PERSONAL IDENTITIES

Description of Personal Characteristics of the Narrator in "Disco Gymnasium"
- Frustrated
- Observant
- Funny
- Strong
- Angry

Description of Personal Characteristics of Donna
- Powerful
- Intimidating
- Unfriendly
- Savvy
- Hard-core

■ 8. Commonalities in social identities and differences in personal identities for "Disco Gymnasium" narrator and Donna in "What Is Bad"

- ■ family structure,
- ■ food,
- ■ socialization values, and
- ■ geographical background.

Yet, these commonalities do not preclude the two women from being unique individuals who have personal traits in common with people who have different social identities. When students outlined these two characters' personal identities, the women's differences as individuals emerged. Social scientists have always struggled with analyzing and documenting powerful commonalities based on social identities that have enormous consequences in our social world and *at the same time* taking into account individuals' uniqueness as displayed in their personal identities.

■ The Creation of Social Identities

There is a severe dichotomy between who I am and who people think I am. I am multiracial; half White, half Black and Filipina. Yet I harbor White privilege: I have my father's blue eyes. When I look in a mirror, does what I see match my heritage? (Yvonne Miller 2001)

Tajfel (1981) argues that the formation of social identities is the consequence of three social psychological processes:

Social categorization: Nationality, language, race, ethnicity, skin color, or any other social or physical characteristics that are meaningful in particular social contexts can be the basis for social categorization by others and, thus, the foundation for the creation of a social identity.

Social comparison: The characteristics of one's group (or groups) such as its status, its richness or poverty, achieve significance *in relation* to perceived differences from other groups and the value connotation attached to those differences.

Psychological work: Psychological work encompasses both cognitive and emotional work that is prompted by what Tajfel assumes is a universal motive: to achieve a positive sense of distinctiveness.

Social Categorization

Any social or physical characteristic that is meaningful in particular life spaces can be the basis for social categorization and therefore the foundation for the creation of social identities. As Yvonne Miller indicates in her essay (see topic highlight 6), others categorize her as white because she inherited her father's phenotype. Her multiracial heritage is not evident in her skin color nor the color of her eyes. The incongruence between the way she looks and her cultural background is something she has to negotiate and resolve. Yvonne asks herself, "How do I want others to see me? How do I see myself? I stare back and consider, carefully, before answering."

Social categorization can lead to stereotyping, but most of the time people use it as a way to orient themselves in their social environments. People rely on social categorization because

- it gives their social world order,
- it makes them feel that they have control over social situations, and
- it helps them make attributions about the causes of behavior, reassuring them that they know their social world.

To illustrate how necessary and powerful social categorization is, consider gender, which is one of the most basic ways in which we categorize

Topic Highlight 6. Reflections on My Altar

by Yvonne Miller, 2001

> If you care about me, you should want to know not only the details of my personal biography but a sense of how race, class, and gender as categories of analysis created the institutional and symbolic backdrop for my personal biography. How can you hope to assess my character without knowing the details of the circumstances I face? (Patricia Hill Collins)

I've been gathering my altar materials for a week now, and setting them aside, one by one, in a corner of my room. Later, as I gazed at the jumbled pile, it struck me that I was subconsciously trying to explain myself: I judged every poem, photo, and memento as a measure of *who I am:* my family, my cultural heritage, my personality, my loves and desires. I found myself turning one of my obsidian owls over and over in the palm of my hand, wondering what I would say when the time came to collapse all my memories and identifications with this owl into a single sentence: This is special to me.

No, no, that's not completely accurate: The owl is special to me, of course, but more in the sense of where I was when I got it (Guatemala; thirteen years old) and its symbolic importance. For me, owls represent the kind of power that comes with gliding silently through dark landscapes—they are sure of themselves; they are brutal in their hunt; they are patient and wise—characteristics that I admire and try to emulate. For these reasons, then, I placed my owls on center stage.

I constructed my altar on the basis of two central questions: who I am and who I pretend to be. These issues are physically manifested in the division of my altar. I placed my various identifiers all around the outside of the box, what I pretend to be; and my secrets are inside the box. The dominant picture is of a drawing that gives me peace and keeps me focused; on the bottom it is inscribed, "the writing on the wall." Alice Walker is there because her writing is truly the one on my own walls: She is one of my first role models. Interestingly enough, most of the people I idolize are women writers: their words give me strength and inspire my own pen.

Encased in two different levels of glass are the images of the people who are most important to me: my mom, my twin brother and little brother, my best friend, and my boyfriend. A picture of my father is absent; this is partly because I couldn't find a photo of him (!) and partly because I truly feel more connected to the other members of my family. I love my dad but I do not believe we could ever be friends.

Inside the box: a blank book. It is a symbol of all my regrets, my shortcomings, and the memories I wish could be erased. It also stands for hope and for the future; my own dream of becoming a writer, and the blank pages that are waiting to be written. Along the edges around the book are propped *National Geographic* magazines; for travel, for the world that I am a part of, and for learning and an open mind.

I loved this project. I felt content and fulfilled as I placed my riches on the altar; doing so forced me to choose what is truly important—or in other words—what is truly important for others to know about me. There is a severe dichotomy between who I am and who people think I am. I am multiracial; half White, half Black and Filipina. Yet I harbor White privilege: I have my father's blue eyes. When I look in a mirror, does what I see match my heritage? Not really, I whisper . . . but right now my reflection is talking: How do you want others to see you? How do you see yourself? I stare back and consider carefully before answering.

Who I am is also what I want. I want to go down fighting for justice. I want my grandmother to talk to me about her life. I want the wide world to look at each other for who they are in ALL of their multiple identities. I want to be accepted by everyone. I want to write.

My philosophy about writing stems from an early association of difference and connectedness: It is important and therapeutic to write about your own experiences; however, to write about others can be a vital source of growth . . . and of power. Those who can skillfully communicate an argument to sway a jury; to relate a story that brings tears out of a well of apathy; to tell the truth through the eyes of a character woven with words . . . I will be frank here: one can never get too sentimental about writers. They can draw blood with exclamation points.

In light of this power of words, a poem by Lucille Clifton is honored on the top part of my altar. Her voice is commanding: "born in Babylon / both nonwhite and woman / what did I see to be except myself?" ■

people. Among the many social cues used to categorize males and females are

- the clothes individuals wear,
- how they move,
- where they go and at what times,
- how they speak,
- what jobs they consider,
- whom they consider for their love objects, and
- decisions about whether or not to have children.

Without using gender as a marker, most people would have difficulty in almost every social interaction. Whether the person is perceived as a man or a woman determines how close people get when speaking to him or her, whether they touch them or not, what topics they broach, and many more things. In fact, soon after a child's sex is known, gender socialization begins. As a study by Judith Bridges (1993) shows, even congratulations cards celebrating the birth of a baby are marked significantly for gender in such a way that the cards for little girls are more often pink and show baby girls in relatively passive poses, whereas the ones for boys are predominantly blue and contain more action (quoted in Franzoi 1996, 142; see figure 9).

Social psychologists make a distinction between **sex** and gender. *Sex* is defined as the biological status of being male or female, whereas *gender* is the meanings that societies and individuals attach to being female or male. Erving Goffman (1987), in his classic study of advertisements in popular magazines, shows that most people need very little information to categorize even a hand as male or female.

Most individuals are so well socialized to categorize by gender that they need only a few cues to make highly accurate assessments (see figure 10). In fact, most children can determine who is a boy and who is a girl fairly early in infancy. Most children also learn *gender constancy*—that is the notion that boys will not biologically turn into girls if they wear a dress or have long hair (and vice versa).

The categorization into male or female (rarely would individuals say both, although it is biologically possible to have genitalia of both sexes) is

■ 9. Birth congratulations cards for boys and girls showing marked gender differences

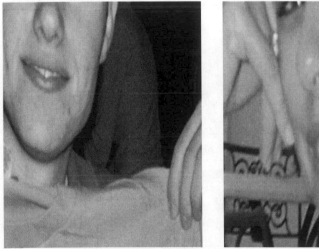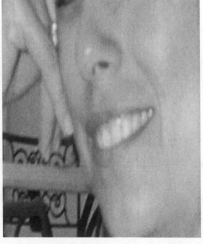

■ 10. Cropped images of a man and a woman, which college students can accurately identify as male and female

based on gender rather than on internal biological characteristics. Most individuals assume congruence of outward gender characteristics (such as dress, voice, and demeanor) with sex. Most of the time, in fact, an individual's biological makeup corresponds to his or her gender, which leads most people to think of gender as synonymous with sex. Most people believe that an individual's sex determines the social aspects of gender.

This distinction, however, does not address sexuality, that is, whether individuals are physically attracted to the opposite sex or to members of their own sex as romantic and sexual objects of desire. It is not uncommon for people to assume the following equation: sex = gender = heterosexuality. When this equation is disturbed, most have difficulty making sense of it. Considerable hostility is directed at individuals who violate this equation, including intersex individuals (i.e., those who have both male and female sexual characteristics and organs), homosexuals, transgendered individuals, and transvestites.

In summary, the determination of individuals' social identities through social categorization is so automatic, learned so early in life, and so persistent in our social world that many people assume these social identities are "natural" categories determined by biology. Many individuals do not recognize the social categories on which social identities are based as socially constructed. Furthermore, individuals arrange a lot of their social behavior around these social categories and attach values to them.

Social Comparison

> My goal for this project was to not reject myself. To not hide myself. And the first thing I looked for was the first thing I was not supposed to do. I looked at other people. Now the logic behind this makes sense. How do we find out about ourselves if we don't look at the environment that we are in? (Marisol Lorenzana 2001)

The second process that underlies the construction of social identities is social comparison. The characteristics of one's group or groups—such as its status and its material wealth or poverty—achieve significance *in relation* to perceived differences from other groups and the value connotations of these differences. As Lorenzana indicates, when she was deciding which social identities to present and highlight in her altar, she looked around to see what other students were doing. Thus, individuals evaluate who they are *in relationship* to others in their environment.

People use social categorization to organize their social world and process information as quickly as possible. That is, individuals observe their environment, and the people in it, and quickly categorize them into the most common social groups. However, not all groups in society are either equally salient or equally important in determining an individual's social position in this country. From a social psychological point of view, the major groups used in social comparison to define a person's social position are:

- race,
- ethnicity,
- class,
- gender,
- sexual orientation, and
- physical ableness.

These social groups, which are used in society to allocate social and economic power, indicate a person's status. The group identities that are most significant in triggering social comparisons are called master statuses. A *master status* is defined as "a socially defined position occupied by a person in society that is very important in shaping her or his self-concept and life choices" (Becker 1963, quoted in Franzoi 1996, 403). Master statuses determine **consensually dominant** and **consensually subordinate groups.**

Individuals who belong to dominant groups have unproblematic social identities because they do not suffer from stigma. Henri Tajfel (1981) proposes that for these groups, their social identities are so natural as to be almost invisible. For example, until very recently being white, male, heterosexual, and rich were desirable statuses, the ideal that others should aspire to, and an identity taken for granted as both natural and normal.

In turn, individuals who are members of historically subordinate groups need to negotiate the stigma attached to their social identities. They have to deal with master statuses that in the eyes of others are less than desirable and make them less worthy as human beings. The reevaluation of their group memberships involves **psychological work** to resist negative social comparisons and achieve positive social identities.

Stigmatized Social Identities: Race, Class, Gender, Sexuality, and Physical Challenges

> The foil is reflective. It is like a mirror; however, this one does not allow for a clear reflection of my physical image. This is significant because as women, for many of us, the strains of society and media prevent us from loving the true image we see in those mirrors. So instead this foil forces me to accept what is there; I must first press out those creases to finally allow myself to clearly see what has always been there. (Emma 2001)

The third process in the creation of social identities involves psychological work, both cognitive and emotional effort which is prompted by what Tajfel assumes is a universal motive—to achieve a positive sense of distinctiveness. That is, all individuals seek to feel good about the groups they belong to. The groups that are most problematic in terms of their members developing a sense of positive distinctiveness—ones that are disparaged, memberships that have to be negotiated frequently because they are visible to others, ones that have become politicized by social movements, and so on—are the most likely to become social identities for individuals. As Emma states in topic highlight 7, women's self-image is problematic when media and society force them to meet unrealistic standards of appearance. She struggles with this image, and her altar was part of negotiating the conflict between what she is supposed to look like and her actual appearance. She has to resolve this incongruence before she can feel positive about self-identifying as a woman. Moreover, it is these identities that become especially powerful psychologically because

- they are easily accessible,
- individuals think a lot about them,
- they are apt to be salient across situations, and
- they are likely to function as schema, frameworks, or social scripts (Gurin, Hurtado, and Peng 1994).

Like Emma, the narrator in "Disco Gymnasium" has to negotiate her self-perception against how others perceive her when she is misidentified as a cleaning lady because she is both a woman and of Mexican descent.

The eighteen inch waist
　　buxom blonde
informs me,
　　"You're late!
　　Bathrooms are a mess!"
I tell her,
　　"No, I'm no cleaning lady
　　I go here, I'm a member."
Her left eyebrow arches
　　with suspicion
she checks my plastic card
　　proof and signature,
　　　　annoyed wave,
　　　　allows me in.

Although the narrator is a member at the fancy gym, the "buxom blonde" assumes that she is there to clean the bathrooms. The narrator and Emma both have social identities—as women, members of the working class, and members of ethnic groups—that are salient across social situations, are visible to others, are not equally valued, and have to be negotiated so they can feel good about belonging to these social groups.

Unproblematic group memberships—ones that are socially valued or accorded privilege, those that are not obvious to others—may not even become social identities. For example, until very recently, being white was not a subject of inquiry and many white people still do not think of it as a social identity (Fine et al. 1997; Hurtado and Stewart 1997; Phinney 1996).

In explaining her altar, Kristin Tillim, a white student in our class (see topic highlight 8) does not mention her race (white), ethnicity (unspecified European), her class background (middle class), or the fact that she has the function of all of her limbs (is physically able). These social identities are unproblematic for her. She doesn't think much about them, they are not particularly salient across social situations, and she does not have to negotiate them to feel good about who she is. The only social identity she seems to negotiate is gender, around which many of her self-doubts about being "good enough" in competence and appearance revolve. So she asserts "Sometimes I think more people would love me (or at least pay attention to me) if I were more like Britney Spears."

Topic Highlight 7. Mi Altar

by Emma, 2001

Every time I drive to that city on a hill my palms begin to sweat and my heart beats so fast I think I'm going to die. The only person I've ever shared this story with is my husband, and I just told him three months ago. Just to think about it I feel rage, shame, and humiliation; it hurts. Today and every day I look around trying to remember where it happened. I can't remember but I want to remember, I have to remember, I need to remember. I know I must find that space so that I can reclaim my "self."

I was seventeen years old, and my friends had invited me to a dance at the university. That night two guys raped me. It happened in the parking lot of one of the colleges. They were nice enough to drive me home. When I was preparing this altar I realized how significant it was to share this by writing about it. I probably won't share it with my group; I don't yet have the courage to do it. But I did tape the definition of the word *rape* on my altar and also a quote from an article I read in *Ms.* The altar is helping me to identify areas in my life that I wish were dead, and it is helping me to remember those things that I thought were buried too deep within my soul. This has been a healing process.

My altar is made from boxes covered with aluminum foil. The boxes are significant because I currently feel like I live in one. Most of my possessions are in boxes; my husband and I rent a room from a family and we only keep those things in our room that we use most often, like clothes and a bed, nothing else fits. So in many ways not only are our things in boxes but we almost technically live in one. The foil is reflective. It is like a mirror; however, this one does not allow for a clear reflection of my physical image. This is significant because as women, for many of us, the strains of society and media prevent us from loving the true image we see in those mirrors. So instead this foil forces me to accept what is there, I must first press out those creases to finally allow myself to clearly see what has always been there.

The pictures of my family are very important to me. There are five pictures. One includes my whole family. My maternal grandmother,

Abuelita Modesta, died two years ago, this picture is of her with her *novio* (boyfriend) Juan. I met her in 1994; she had the warmest hands and the saddest eyes. There are two black-and-white pictures; they are my mom and dad as teenagers. The other pictures are of my whole family, and then one of Anthony and me. We got married last year. I dedicate the mini altar to my family. I wish for the troubles that haunt us to be dead and buried. I wish for us to only revisit them in memory.

Much of who I am today I owe to my mom and dad. From my mother I have learned about my love of family and my love for food. My mom is an amazing cook; she can make something out of nothing. For her in my altar I have the *frijoles, chiles de árbol* and the ceramic *nopal* (beans, chiles, and prickly pear pads). From my father I have learned about the desire for knowledge and the love of writing poetry. My dad and I often exchange books that we know only have meaning to us, and we share our poetry; he mainly writes *corridos* [ballads or poems based on actual events]. The *ristra de chiles rojos* [string of red chiles] is for him. We used to make them together.

I worked for ten and a half years at the Santa Cruz Women's Health Center. I feel very fortunate to have had that experience. My name tag is in my altar as a symbol of pride and honor for having served and met so many wonderful women and children.

The little red Volkswagen bug is there because up until last year I used to drive a 1972 red bug. Her name was "Tut Put" and she was very special to me. The wood elephant does not mean that I am a Republican. Elephants represent strength and integrity. I have been collecting them since I was a child.

There are two Frida Kahlo images. One, *Unos cuantos piquetitos*, represents the struggle my family has with domestic violence. I dedicate that image to all the women who have died and suffered due to those crimes to their bodies. The other Frida Kahlo painting is called *Las dos Fridas*. This represents the duality that as Mexicanas [Mexican women] we are destined to struggle with. We are both *indígena* [Indian] and Spanish. This goes along with the clippings of what we call ourselves and what others call us. It is my way of reclaiming and accepting my culture. The little picture between the Frida Kahlo paintings represents the weight we must carry in order to be who we are. The altar itself is me; all of me, the bad and the good, and only my shoulders can carry the weight. ■

Topic Highlight 8. Untitled

by Kristin Tillim, 2001

Altars have always been markers in my life. This altar, being part of a project and part of this class, makes it that much more significant because it is part of something bigger than myself. My altar is built around the concept of what I am afraid of and what I keep hidden. I am afraid of showing myself and not feeling validated. I am afraid of not being worthy enough to show myself in the first place, so this project is a way for me to look at those fears and build the altar anyway.

The altar is divided into two spaces—what I am afraid of and what I am not, what I want to show people and what I want to keep hidden, what I want to be and what I am. The bottom half of the altar is what I am and what I keep hidden. It is my safe space. The photograph of my grandmother, mother, sister, and myself is the center of my hidden half. This picture was the last picture taken of my grandmother, and it was taken on the last day I was with my grandmother. A few weeks after this picture was taken, she fell into a coma and died. I was with her, holding her hand, when she died. My grandmother and my mother are the two most important people in my life. The picture of my mother and me in the pumpkin patch reminds me of the time in my life, probably the best time, when it was just the two of us, before my mother married my father. The pumpkin patch is important as well. Fall and especially Halloween are my favorite times of the year. It is when I feel the most connected to myself.

I used the deep box and the dark cool colors on the bottom box because it feels like I could hide inside of it. It is a space where I am not judged, where no one can decide who I am. The railway ticket and postcard are reminders of where I have been and where I can go. The postcard is a scene of Williamsport, Pennsylvania. I was born in California, but lived in Pennsylvania and Oklahoma for five years. Living away from California made me see who I was. Change in location allowed parts of myself that were not essential to fall away, leaving a raw core. The signs on the outer flaps of the box are voodoo signs that mean ascent of the mind. Learning and growing keep me sane and keep me alive. If I am not transforming my mind, I cannot breathe. The picture on the base of the box is a CD jacket cover of the soundtrack to the movie *Hedwig and the Angry Inch*. I cannot describe how deeply important this movie is to me. Hedwig's courage and strong vulnerability put my life in perspective. As Hedwig says, "You're such a sissy. What are you afraid of, what are you afraid of, huh?" Fear dominates my life. The movie has made me see this and has taught me to love myself without being scared. And the sound-track is great.

The top half of the altar is the part of myself I fear. Like the box, this part of myself is raw and vulnerable. It is on the top because right now, this is what dominates my thoughts and actions. Writing is so important to me, but painful as well. I want more than anything to be a good writer. I have never been satisfied with anything I have written. The writing on the back of the box are pieces of the most significant poems I have written. The torn prints on either side of the poems are prints of Toulouse-Lautrec paintings. He is my favorite artist. I want to live in the world he paints. I am drawn to the eerie carnivalesque and the strange beauty. Yet I feel that I am not beautiful enough to be a part of that. The entire top half of the altar revolves around my feelings of not being good enough. I am not good enough to write, to have my picture taken, to be a photographer, to own a nice perfume. I am so afraid that I will never be good enough.

The red cloth is a piece of the curtain from my high school stage. Acting was a big part of my identity. I no longer act because the bad experiences started outweighing the good. Or maybe it is that I do not feel that I am good enough to act. The photograph of the woman sitting on the bed is of the poet Diane Di Prima. I want to have her talent, strength, genius, and utter fabulousness. I love her writing, but she re-minds me of what I am not. The small bag is full of worry dolls because I worry all the time. The pink lace is a symbol of my sexuality. I am not pink'lace'sweet'sexy. I feel too hard, too severe. Sometimes I think more people would love me (or at least pay attention to me) if I were more like Britney Spears. The black rope symbolizes how bound I am to these fears and how trapped. I had to make the whole altar glittery because life is better when there is glitter in it. ■

Identification and Consciousness in Ethnic Identity Formation

I have a shirt similar to the one in the picture; my grandmother gave it to me, and said that it was made by the Tarascan Indians in Michoacán. Those Indians are my ancestors. (Claudia E. Mojica 2001)

Tajfel's social identity theory, which has been elaborated extensively by others, provides a sophisticated framework for understanding how individuals make sense of their group memberships—both unproblematic ones and those that are stigmatized. However, Tajfel's theory does not elaborate how individuals become aware of other groups in the environment and on what basis they make judgments about the inferiority or superiority of their group memberships. Patricia Gurin and her colleagues (1980) provide a theoretical bridge by making a distinction between **identification** and **consciousness.** According to their elaboration, most people are aware of their social identities. For example, almost universally everybody can tell whether they are female or male, whether they are Chicana/o or white, whether they are poor, middle class, or wealthy, and whether or not they are physically challenged. But according to Gurin and her colleagues, individuals are less likely to be aware of how individuals in that category, as a group, rate in relationship to other groups in the same life space—that is, they may be highly identified but not at all conscious of their entire stratum or group. *Consciousness* refers to whether individuals are aware that the groups they belong to hold a certain status (either powerful or not powerful) in society and whether they decide to take action to change this status, not just for themselves, but for other members of the group as well (Gurin, Miller, and Gurin 1980). For example, an individual may have a very high identification with being Mexican but not be conscious that other groups discriminate against Mexicans as a group. For example, Claudia Mojica in topic highlight 9 strongly identifies with her Mexican Indian heritage, but it is not clear from her essay whether she is conscious of the status implications of that identification.

In many ways, the theoretical distinction between identification and consciousness helps to explain the relatively low incidence of individuals who call themselves Chicanos/as. Arturo González defines a Chicano/a as "a person of Mexican descent living in the United States. The term emphasizes pride in the Mexican American culture, history, and indigenous roots, as well as an interest in activism" (González 2002, 131). Calling oneself

Chicano/a by definition implies consciousness—that is, awareness that members of this group are unfairly treated in a discriminatory manner and furthermore that the discrimination is group based, rather than stemming from personality or individual characteristics. This theoretical distinction also helps explain why the Chicano/a identity occurs mostly among educated people of Mexican descent: They are the most likely to have studied the conditions of discrimination and have come to their consciousness through intellectual development and understanding of intergroup relations.

To summarize, social identity, which consists of one's group memberships and the emotional attachment one has for these group memberships, is largely derived through social comparison. The meaning of one's group—its value, its significance, and so on—is largely based on what other groups are present in the environment. When different values are attached to different group memberships, people have to do psychological work to come to terms with their social identities. Tajfel posits that individuals strive not only to be different from other groups, but to be different in a positive way. We now review a possible framework for understanding the differences in identification depending on whether individuals have both identification and consciousness versus only identification (see figure 11).

An Example of Identification and Consciousness

We will use the characters in Gregory Nava's film *Mi Familia/My Family* to illustrate several examples, by no means a comprehensive exposition, of variations in ethnic identification and consciousness using Tajfel's framework and Gurin and her colleagues' (1980) elaboration of social identity theory. *Mi Familia* depicts the history of the Sánchez family from the 1920s, when they immigrate to Los Angeles from Mexico, to the 1980s. (See topic highlight 10 for a summary of the film.)

The Sánchez family has six children, and in the film we see them grow up into adulthood taking on different adaptations to their ethnic identity (see topic highlight 11).

José and María Sánchez: Identification Only

In the final scene of the film, José and María Sánchez, who are now in their seventies, are sitting in their dining room drinking coffee and enjoying the afternoon sun filtering through the kitchen windows. They have raised

by Claudia E. Mojica, 2001

> The aim of life is to live, and to live means to be aware, joyously, drunkenly, serenely, divinely aware. (Henry Miller)

Tomorrow is already at the heels of today, and with it brings a world of new opportunities and situations. The importance of my altar is not so much what is in it, but the colors used to represent aspects of my life. There is so much newness for me here, every time I take a moment to stop and listen, I am bombarded with a strange sensation of familiarity.

The painting is the central part of my altar. It depicts a girl in a meadow somewhere, flying a red kite. The girl wears what seems to be a jean skirt and a cream-colored peasant shirt. I have a shirt similar to the one in the picture; my grandmother gave it to me, and said that it was made by the Tarascan Indians in Michoacán. Those Indians are my ancestors. The kite in the picture is red . . . red for courage. The wind that picks up the kite represents the flight of new ideas that are currently a powerful force in my life. Balancing the kite is like a dance, like striking a deal with the forces of gravity that are active in their attempts to ground the kite. The girl in the image, however, manages a steady hold of the kite, and seems successful at balancing it between the two opposing forces. I figure that the new ideas, or the wind, is coming from all of the literature, and from the excitement of knowing that there are other women like me . . . not just out there, but in my own classroom. Gravity is the dominant culture, and my family. . . . I feel grounded by both expressing fear of too much change. The state of balance represents a state of identity. . . . I'm getting closer to knowing who I am.

The corn at the sides is representative of my family. I come from a long line of farmers. They were farmers in Mexico, and then moved to become farmers of the fields in California. The blue ocean candle is representative of my brother, he sent it to me after he went away, on his own journey to find himself. The poem about sisters is self-explanatory. . . . She has been one of my biggest motivators, and for that I love her. The white blanket at the base was made by my mother, and it is a symbolic of a blank slate. An entirely new opportunity to re-create myself. The burgundy flowers wrapped in white cotton are symbolic of those aspects of my personality that are evolving. The flowers are symbolic of visiting the dead, and taking flowers to their graves. In a way this altar serves as a grave for the old ways I am shedding, and have shed. The little book of Zen was the beginning of reaffirming my faith in my higher power. I don't believe in religion, but I do believe in God. Catholicism continues to be important to me, but not for religious reasons, for the church, and for that reason I continue to call myself Catholic. I am as much Catholic as I am Mexican.

The thin veil over the picture is symbolic of my guarded nature. Though it may seem that I am open and inviting, I am mostly not. The walls are getting thinner, and the access is being granted with more frequency . . . but the fact is that I am still guarded. The flowers among the burgundy, and cream-colored pieces of material are symbolic of my belief of inter-being with nature. Leaves and flowers both hang over the thin veil that protects me, and that is because I see that though I feel some-what disconnected at times, I still realize that I am part of the "big picture" of life.

This altar's stillness represents my current state. This is my time, my life, my field, and my own blue skies. In it I am free to recreate myself, and my life, as I best see fit. The grassy open field, and the never-ending skies show the vast potential for greatness in my life. Life is like a dream, loosely held together by the details of the day. ■

their six children, all of whom have moved out to live their own lives and raise their children. As José and María contemplate their accomplishments, José turns to his wife and says, "We've had a good life. . . . It is wrong to wish for too much in this life. God has been good to us. We've been lucky. And our life, it has been very, very, good." María replies, "You're right. We've had a very good life." Both have worked hard all their lives, never comparing themselves to the whites who live across the bridge in the affluent parts of Los Angeles. Although José worked for many years as a gardener in these homes owned mostly by wealthy whites, he does not feel cheated because he is Mexican. Things just turned out the way they did,

Topic Highlight 10. Plot summary of *Mi Familia*

The film *Mi Familia* is the epic tale of José Sanchez's family over the course of five generations. Paco, the film's narrator, tells the story of the year-long migration of his father José Sánchez from Central Mexico to southern California. José Sanchez arrives in East Los Angeles in the 1920s and stays with his uncle, "El Californio," who was born in this area when it was still part of Mexico. José finds a job, with his uncle's help, as a gardener for white families living across the river from the Mexican part of town. José meets María, who works as a nanny for one of these well-to-do families, and they fall in love and marry. Two years later they have two daughters, Irene and Antonia.

During the Depression, it was customary for the Immigration and Naturalization Service (INS) to conduct raids in predominantly Chicano communities and deport people of Mexican descent, whether they were "illegals" or U.S. citizens. María, a U.S. citizen, who was pregnant with her third child, was caught in one of the INS raids and deported to Mexico. María was able to stay with her aunt in a small Mexican town until she gave birth to Chucho. María struggled to get back to her family in East Los Angeles, enduring a long trek by foot and almost losing Chucho while crossing a treacherous river on a rickety barge. María eventually reunited with the rest of her family in the United States.

Through the years, José and María have three more children, Paco, Memo, and Jimmy. Each of their children takes a different path in life, some successful, others not so successful.

As a teenager, Chucho accidentally kills a rival gang member in a knife fight at a school dance. Jimmy, who is almost ten years younger than Chucho, adores and idolizes Chucho. The night of the killing, two young policemen see Chucho and shoot him in cold blood, as Jimmy watches in shock.

Some years later, Antonia, who has taken vows as a nun, comes home for a visit. The family is shocked when she announces she has left the convent and has married a former priest, who also has left his order. Antonia and her husband, David, open a nonprofit organization to help Latinos/as with their immigration and other problems. Around the same time, Jimmy has grown up and is incarcerated for dealing marijuana. Shortly after his release from prison, Antonia tries to persuade him to marry Isabel, an undocumented Salvadoran, who is about to be deported. Antonia tells Jimmy that the marriage is only a paper document to save Isabel, who is likely to be killed if she returns to her country because of her father's union sympathies. Jimmy reluctantly agrees, but over time Jimmy and Isabel become good friends, and eventually lovers. Isabel becomes pregnant and Jimmy turns over a new leaf, going to work to support his family. Isabel dies during childbirth and is survived by their son, Carlitos. When Jimmy, grieving for his wife, refuses to have anything to do with his son, José and María take in Carlitos and raise him. After a few years Jimmy repents, and after a great deal of heartache, Jimmy and Carlitos finally become a family. ■

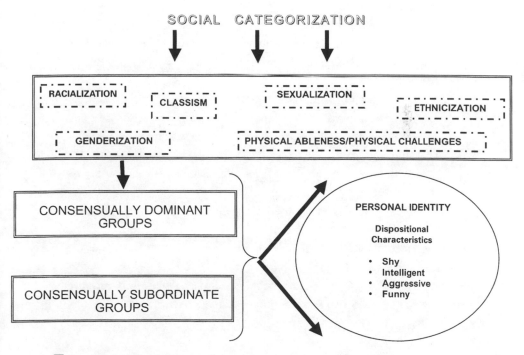

■ 11. The conceptual difference between personal and social identities

Topic Highlight 11. **Identity Adaptations of the Characters in *Mi Familia* to Dominant and Subordinate Group Status**

José and María (the parents): *identification only,* are happy to do the best they can with their lives

Chucho: involved with drug dealing, the rebel, *identification and* **consciousness,** no **cognitive alternatives,** deviance to cope with stigma

Jimmy: younger brother and admirer of Chucho, appears later in the movie after he has been released from prison (a.k.a. Jimbo), *identification and consciousness, no cognitive alternatives,* deviance to cope with stigma, until he undergoes a transformation of consciousness and decides to reform himself for the sake of his son

Memo: studious, later attends UCLA Law School and denies his Mexican heritage (a.k.a. William, Bill, Guillermo), *identification and consciousness, with cognitive alternatives;* he sees assimilation into the dominant group as a solution to stigma

Antonia: becomes a nun but later leaves her order to marry an ex-priest and is the activist in the family (a.k.a. carnala, Toni), *identification and consciousness, with cognitive alternatives,* collective group action to cope with stigma

David: Antonia's husband, an activist ex-priest, *identification and consciousness, with cognitive alternatives,* collective group action to cope with what he perceives as illegitimate privileges accorded him as an educated white man

Karen Gillespie: Memo's fiancée, *identification only,* is happy with her status

The Gillespies (Karen's parents): from Beverly Hills, *identification only,* are happy with their status

Irene: second oldest sister, who is married and owns a restaurant, *identification only,* is happy with her status

Paco (narrator): a writer, *identification and consciousness, with cognitive alternatives,* collective group action to cope with stigma ▪

and both he and his wife are happy with what they have accomplished. They know they are Mexican and working class; they feel pride in their background and have taught their children about their heritage; they do not make intergroup comparisons with non-Mexicans, especially whites, or with individuals who are better off than they are.

Chucho Sánchez: Identification and Consciousness, No Cognitive Alternatives to Group Stigma

In comparison with José and María, their son Chucho feels very differently about the power differentials between Mexicans and whites and how that contributes to his feelings of frustration.

In the scene reproduced in topic highlight 12, José confronts his teen-age son after the police call the house and tell him that Chucho has been caught selling drugs. As Chucho enters the house, José asks him, "Where have you been?" and Chucho replies "Out." An argument ensues, which culminates in José recriminating his son for selling *mota* (marijuana) and not having any dignidad (dignity). Chucho replies in anger that money is what earns people respect in the United States and that he does not want to be like his family or any other working-class Mexican.

Chucho identifies as Mexican but knows that being Mexican implies limited opportunities for success. He believes neither in the legitimacy of the system nor that it is likely to change. In other words, Chucho does not perceive cognitive alternatives to the existing power differentials between groups. Chucho's solution to his discomfort with existing power differential is to rebel by violating the law and getting money, regardless of the consequences.

Antonia Sánchez: Identification and Consciousness, with Cognitive Alternatives to Group Stigma

Chucho's sister Antonia identifies with her ethnic heritage and, like Chucho, is skeptical of the legitimacy of the power differential between groups in U.S. society. However, unlike Chucho, who engages in individual unlawful behavior, Antonia sees the system as unstable and amenable to change through collective political action. That is, Antonia perceives cognitive alternatives to the existing power differential between groups. Antonia decides to become a nun and travels to Central America to do missionary work. During her stay there, she becomes politicized around immigration issues, leaves her order, and marries an ex-priest, David,

Topic Highlight 12. Identity Adaptation of Chucho Sánchez to Subordinate Group Status

Chucho (*entering the house*): *Hola, Jefe* [Hi, Boss].

José (*sitting in the living room*): Where have you been, huh?

Chucho: Out

José: Out? What does that mean?

Chucho: It means out.

José: You're out of school now. Are you looking for a job?

Chucho: No, I am not. I got money, Jefe.

José: Where do you get this money?

Chucho: I just get it, that's all.

José: Selling mota [grass]? Is that it? Selling mota? (*grabs Chucho*) . . .

Chucho: What difference does it make? . . .

José: The police called here tonight. *La policía*. I didn't raise my children to be *sinvergüenzas delincuentes* [shameless delinquents]. I, I, when I came here, walking all the way from Michoacán, and what your mother went through to bring you back when you were a baby so you could grow up to be a man with respect. Don't you have any pride? Look at your sister Irene and your brother Paco—in the Navy! . . . *Pero tú* [but you], selling marijuana like some hoodlum! *No tienes conciencia, no tienes dignidad!* [You have no conscience, you have no dignity.]

Chucho: Fuck la dignidad! Fuck it! And fuck your struggle! You think anybody cares about it here? Huh? This, this is all they respect in this country (*showing him a wad of money*). And it don't matter how you get it, as long as you get it. I don't want to be like no Mexican. Uh uh. If you think for one minute I want to spend all fucking day pulling up weeds and mowing lawns, you have another think coming, *a la chingada con eso* [fuck that]. I don't want to be like Irene. I don't want to be like Paco. And most of all, I don't want to be like you! ■

whom she met in her travels. They both return to Los Angeles to work for an organization in East Los Angeles that helps undocumented workers from Central America gain political asylum. In a critical scene in the film, Antonia is trying to convince Jimmy, her brother who has just completed a prison sentence for robbery, to marry Isabel Magaña, a Salvadoran who has been working as a maid and is on the verge of being deported (see topic highlight 13). Antonia tells Jimmy, who is a U.S. citizen, that marrying Isabel would be a way to get back at the system responsible for imprisoning him.

Antonia identifies herself as of Mexican descent, but she also recognizes that members of her ethnic group are treated differently than whites. Furthermore, her consciousness of the power differential between whites and Mexicans helps her understand other groups in similar subordinated positions. She extends her political solidarity to other Latinos/as, including the Salvadoran undocumented worker whom she is trying to save from deportation and probable persecution because of her father's unionizing efforts.

Memo Sánchez, Identification and Consciousness, with Cognitive Alternatives to Group Stigma

Memo, the youngest brother, also identifies himself as of Mexican descent and is conscious about the power differential between whites and Mexican descendants. However, he believes the difference in power is legitimate and stable (see topic highlight 14). His solution to experiencing less power than other groups is to exit his group and strive to assimilate by studying hard and succeeding as a lawyer. He attends law school at the University of California, Los Angeles, where he meets his fiancée, Karen Gillespie, a wealthy, white fellow law student whose family resides in an affluent part of Los Angeles. Memo brings the Gillespie family to meet his own family in East Los Angeles. Although the Gillespie family have been longtime residents of the city, they have never crossed the river to East Los Angeles, and they are surprised by the cultural differences around food, language, and social etiquette. As just one example, Memo has changed his name from Guillermo (Memo is his nickname) to Bill. The Gillespie family looks perplexed when "Bill's" family calls him Memo, which he tries to explain: "They call me Memo—my family calls me that. It is diminutive for Guillermo. That's William in Spanish. Memo is like Bill, see?"

Memo exemplifies those group members who have identified and are conscious, but because they feel the existing power differential between groups

Topic Highlight 13. Identity Adaptation of Antonia Sánchez to Subordinate Group Status

Antonia enters the house, where she finds Jimmy sitting on the couch, watching TV and fixing a lamp.

Antonia: Hey, Jimmy, how's parole treating you?

Jimmy: Hey, *carnala* [sis]. What are you doing here?

Antonia: Where're Mom and Dad?

Jimmy: Mom's at church, you know. Dad's mowing lawns. . . . How's shit over there at your office, huh?

Antonia: Tough. We had this case come in yesterday—young girl from El Salvador—she's been picked up by immigration. We've been able to trace where she is, but if we don't come up with something fast, she is going to be deported. Her father was a union organizer. . . . So, if she's lucky, she will end up in jail. But probably she'll end up dead. David and I put our brains together—

Jimmy: Well, that's a whole lot of brains between the two of you. I am sure you'll come up with something.

Antonia: Yeah, well, you know, we were thinking that if we could say she was engaged to someone from here—you know, a citizen—we could get her out. I mean, I know it is a long shot—

Jimmy: Nah, nah, nah, that will never work. La Migra is not that dumb.

Antonia: You'd be surprised, they really are that dumb. Plus, I think we could make a good enough case. Of course we got to find someone who'd agree to marry her. . . . We'd, we, uh, have to prove that an actual wedding took place, in order to pull it off. And we'd have to find someone today. . . .

Jimmy: Forget it. Like I said, it's a bad idea. . . . Well, even if La Migra is dumb enough to buy it—like you say—put that up there (*hanging lamp*) —you still need the guy. Right? . . . You still need this famous *baboso* [dimwit] citizen who is going to marry this girl. There's nobody stupid enough to do that. . . . (*Looks at the lamp and realizes that Antonia is looking at him.*) Wait a minute—wait a fucking minute here. Is that why you came over? To ask me to marry this fucking Lucha?

Antonia: I know it's a lot to ask. . . . Somebody's life is at stake.

Jimmy: My life is at stake. Did you get your brains all screwed up with that political bullshit of yours?

Antonia: Look, if you just stopped being so emotional for a minute, you'd see that it's not that big of a deal.

Jimmy: Not that big of a deal? You know, that's your problem. You've always been real bossy ever since we were little; you always knew what was best for everyone. You know what you are? You're a fucking control freak, that's what you are.

Antonia: Well, you've always been a big *pendejo* [idiot], so what? . . . Look, all I am asking is for you to put your name on a piece of paper and save a girl's life. That's all. . . . I am just asking you to sign a piece of paper. . . . Look, I am not asking for you to live with her. . . . Or have babies or anything like that. Just go through the motions for me, Jimmy.

Jimmy: Go through the motions? You're talking about marriage, carnala, marriage. That's out!

Antonia: When did you become so bourgeois, huh?

Jimmy: Hey, fuck you, and don't you ever call me bourgeois again, carnala. Whatever the fuck that means.

Antonia: Look Jimmy, all it is really is signing your names and saying "I do." That's it. Listen to me. And if it saves one girl's life, then why not, huh? You and I know the system is worth for shit. We know that. So we use the system to fuck up the system. That's what I say.

Jimmy: You're really starting to piss me off, carnala. You know you got a way of putting things—

Antonia: *Es la pura verdad.* [It's the pure truth.]

Jimmy: Who are you to tell me what the fucking truth is? . . .

Antonia: Just listen to me for a minute, huh. Will you just relax, please? . . . Look. This could be your way of getting back at them. Every cop, guard, judge—the whole system. Just, just think about it. With this one little act you could say "Fuck you" to the whole establishment. If I were a man, I would do it. ■

Topic Highlight 14. **Identity Adaptation of Memo Sánchez to Subordinate Group Status**

Memo brings his fiancée, Karen Gillespie, and her parents, Mr. and Mrs. Gillespie, to his family's house in East Los Angeles. They all enter the Sánchez household, where all of Memo's siblings are present.

Memo: Here we are.

Mrs. Gillespie: Oh, this is lovely. . . .

José: We have been wanting to meet you. (*Everyone is socializing*)

María: It is so nice to have you here. José and I are very proud to have you in our home. Welcome.

Memo's Family: Salud

The Gillespies: Cheers

María: Memo always tells us so much about you.

Mrs. Gillespie: Who?

Memo: They call me Memo—my family calls me that. It is diminutive for Guillermo. That's William in Spanish. Memo is like Bill, see?

Everyone: Bill

Mrs. Gillespie: That's cute. That is cute.

Mr. Gillespie: Well, Karen certainly has told us a lot about you folks.

María: Oh, yes.

Mr. Gillespie: Bill, don't you have a younger brother?

Memo's Family: You mean Jimbo, he's around here. Jimbo!

María: This is my son, Jimmy.

Mrs. Gillespie: Bill told us you were away at school.

Jimmy: School? Not exactly school. . . .

Antonia: Actually, he was in prison for a little while.

Mr. Gillespie: Prison?

Jimmy: I read a lot of books though—that's what he must have meant.

Karen Gillespie: Mother, it's just one of those things that can happen, it's not Bill's fault.

Mrs. Gillespie Oh, I know. ∎

is legitimate and stable, opt for assimilation into the dominant group. They reject the values, culture, and language of their subordinate group. Memo/Guillermo/Bill chooses individual assimilation as the solution to his stigmatized social identity as a working-class Chicano son of immigrants.

In summary, subordinate group members who both have identified and are conscious but feel the existing power differential between groups is *illegitimate* can opt for either rebellion or deviance as a way to defy the status quo. Chucho and Jimmy both turn to selling drugs and robbery as solutions to their lack of power resulting from their stigmatized social identities as working-class Chicanos of immigrant parents. In contrast, Antonia, although skeptical of the legitimacy of the system, chooses instead of individual deviance collective action on behalf of her group to retain a positive sense of self about being Chicana.

Political Consciousness and the Renunciation of Privilege

Tajfel's social identity theory also makes predictions about dominant group members and their social identity adaptations. This is important because it contrasts with previous scholarship on **acculturation** and **assimilation.** Although that body of literature recognizes the possibility that different ethnic groups would be affected when they came in contact with each other, in the research on assimilation and acculturation, the process was described as unidirectional. The minority "ethnic group" changes to become more like what is variously called the "dominant," "mainstream," or "white" group. This type of approach effectively ignores ways that cultural contact can indeed bring change in both the subordinate and the dominant groups.

In *Mi Familia* we have an example of a dominant group member, Antonia's husband David, who identifies as white and male but believes that the power these social identities give him is not "natural" and should be challenged. He renounces the privileges of his dominant social identities and joins the subordinate group in its struggle for social justice. He rejects the priesthood, marries Antonia, learns Spanish, and joins her as a coworker in a political organization fighting for immigrant rights. He questions the legitimacy of the system and sees it as unstable enough to be changeable through political action. Tajfel's model can incorporate this kind of adaptation, whereas in their conventional usage acculturation and assimilation models cannot.

◼ Summary

In this chapter we delineated what social identity is, how it is formed, and how it differs from group consciousness:

- Social identity is the part of an individual's self-concept that derives from his or her recognition of belonging to categories and groups, along with the value and emotional significance attached to those memberships.

- Social categorization, the process of putting individuals into categories, initiates the formation of social identity. Nationality, language, race, ethnicity, skin color, or any other social or physical characteristic, can be the basis for social categorization and thus the foundation for the construction of a social identity.

- The categories that are most important in shaping a person's self-concept and life choices are called *master statuses*. Master statuses include race, ethnicity, social class, gender, sexual orientation, and physical challenges.

- Social comparison is the next step in the formation of social identity. Once individuals are categorized, they tend to compare the groups to which they belong with other groups in society. The status and relative wealth of one's groups achieve significance in relation to perceived differences from other groups, and in relation to the value placed on those differences.

- Individuals who belong to privileged, high-status groups have unproblematic identities because their groups give them a positive sense of distinctiveness. Individuals who belong to less privileged, subordinate groups have to negotiate the stigma associated with them.

- The negotiation of stigma requires cognitive and emotional psychological work aimed at achieving a positive sense of distinctiveness. That work involves what we are calling group consciousness: awareness of the group's status and the discrimination it faces, a judgment about the legitimacy or illegitimacy of the group's status, and a decision regarding whether or not to try to change this status for oneself and for the group.

- The characters in *Mi Familia* exhibit this psychological work. They show various ways in which individuals experiencing a similar situation may adapt to their groups statuses.

by Xochitl Gutierrez

What was once a meaningless shoebox, covered in green floral fabric, was suddenly transformed into an abundance of history. Item by item, Teri slowly lifted objects from her backpack, describing the importance of its place found in her identity altar. An old nametag from her past employment with the Bank of America, held the sole reason for her being at UCSC. She explained the frustration and dissatisfaction the job engulfed her in, making her want to become something more than just a minimum-wage employee. Each object held more than a story, but a reason why she is where she is today.

Her choice to be candid with our group, who were all strangers to her, proved to be truly effective in her ability to explain her life history. A pre-teen picture of herself expressed her desire once more to regain the title of her innocence. The deep regret she has for losing her innocence at such a young age leaves her with sadness and disappointment. She shared the family secret of alcoholism, it being common in her family, which was objectified by a picture of a vodka bottle. She is now proud to admit that she is a recovering alcoholic.

Family was central in her presentation. She pulled out a picture of her grandmother, who has long passed away, as being the person who gave her strength and inspiration to utilize her voice and fight for her passions. A picture of bright red jalapeños symbolized the love for her mother's skill at preparing Mexican meals and Teri's inability to do the same because of countless disastrous attempts.

It was through Teri's openness that I was able to make connections to my life. Her altar brought back many memories I had growing up. Her enjoyment of playing a Mexican game called *la lotería* shot back vivid memories of when my family would sit around the kitchen table and play the same game. It was in her ability to share her identity through oral histories. Lectures and course readings continue to stress the importance of verbally preserving your history. As is evident in Teri's presentation, she is holding onto her history through the words of each object placed inside the altar she constructed.

Teri found that by expressing her identity through personal tragedies, and at the same time successes, she was able to present a touching altar presentation. I appreciated the fact that each object had a story, detailed and interesting, she never rushed her explanations, and I found this a factor in why her altar stood out to me long after her presentation. Teri allowed the audience a peek into very dark and deep stories in her life that I could not have asked of anything more. I found Teri's honesty and ability to share her history was commendable and very much appreciated. ■

- Members of privileged, high-status groups sometimes engage in this psychological work also. Not all of them simply accept their privilege as natural and unproblematic. *Mi Familia* includes an example of this adaptation as well.

In the next chapter we examine the role of group life in creating and maintaining personal and social identity, and in making it possible for these two aspects of identity to be integrated into a positive sense of self.

■ Discussion Exercises

1. With a group of students, watch Lourdes Portillo's film *La Ofrenda*. This film is available in most university libraries or can be obtained through interlibrary loan.

2. Discuss why the cultural practice of building altars as part of the Día de los Muertos celebration may have significance for Chicanos/as and other Latinos/as in the United States.

3. Construct your own social identity altar using objects such as photographs, cards, letters, books, art pieces, or anything that visually explains who you are and what groups you belong to.

4. Meet in your group again to present your altar and explain the significance of each object.

5. Write a one-page essay, similar to the ones included in this chapter, to explore what you learned about yourself and your background through constructing the altar.

6. Pick one student in your group and write a one-page paper on what you learned about that person and about his or her history and background (see "Altar Response," in topic highlight 15).

7. Exchange these papers with others in your group and read them aloud. Be sure to discuss any issues that come up, either after each paper is read or after all the papers have been read.

Language, Culture, and Community

Group Life in Creating and
Maintaining Identities

¡La Cultura Cura! (Culture cures, a popular slogan of the Chicano Movement)

In the last chapter we examined the different ways individuals can respond to having stigmatized **social identities;** these social adaptations include choosing to abandon their subordinate group and assimilate to the dominant group, becoming involved in individual deviance, or engaging in political action to dismantle the power differential between groups. According to Tajfel (1981) dominant group members can also choose whether to question or accept their superiority. Some dominant group members accept the status quo, while others create distance between themselves and subordinate group members, for example by promoting separatist ideologies or organizations like the Aryan Brotherhood, the Ku Klux Klan, or Save Our Borders. Still other dominant group members may renounce their group privilege and join the subordinate group in their struggles for social justice. These dominant group members may even transculturate into the subordinate group through marriage or by learning the subordinate group's language and culture.

All of these adaptations, however, are based on an individual's perceptions of his or her group memberships. French social psychologist Erika Apfelbaum (1979) has expanded Tajfel's theory of individual adaptations by proposing that stigma also works at the group level. The three social mechanisms Apfelbaum proposes, which we will discuss in this chapter, are meritocracy, the establishment of the universal rule, and degrouping. We then proceed to review how groups can gain positive views of their group memberships through political empowerment and reclaiming their history, language, culture, and art.

Meritocracy

According to the theory of social mobility, members of the subordinated (group)[1] may climb the ladder up the social hierarchy if they simply fulfill all the universally required conditions. (Apfelbaum 1979, 199)

"Work hard and you'll succeed," I heard. And so I did. (Roa 2003)

Apfelbaum theorizes that most Western democracies function under the ideology of a **meritocracy.** Rewards are ostensibly not accorded by individuals' group memberships (class, ethnicity, race, or **gender**). Instead, all individuals from all groups are judged by the same standards that define who is meritorious and who is not.

In other words, a meritocracy is distinctly different from a class-based society like that of the United Kingdom where, at least historically, class background—let's say royalty—incurs certain rewards simply on the basis of family lineage. Class pervades all of society, such that the closer an individual's familial relationship to royalty (e.g., first cousin versus second cousin to the royal family), the more access he or she has to privilege. Royals were believed to have descended from God and therefore to deserve veneration. Individual actions or "merits" have no relationship to their God-given privilege, thereby exempting royalty from the rules followed by the common folk. Another counterexample to a meritocracy is a caste system, which is another type of class-based society. In India, the caste into which a person is born determines the specific privileges to which he or she is entitled. At the bottom of the social system is a caste known as the "untouchables." The caste system is related to wealth and determines what professions an individual can enter. For example, untouchables cannot be doctors or lawyers or practice other high-prestige professions; historically, they performed tasks considered "unclean," such as handling the dead.

Universal Rule

Thus, we have a "universal rule" said to apply equally to both groups in the relation; whereas, in fact, the "one law for everybody" idea is supported by a series of social mechanisms and institutions at the disposal only of the dominant group. (Apfelbaum 1979, 199)

[T]he wound healed
in the shape of my Americanness

My 22nd year the truth was revealed to me
"White man is on top"
"And you? Sorry, honey, you're somewhere near
the bottom"

(Roa 2003)

According to Apfelbaum (1979), meritocracies have a **universal rule** that defines the conditions for achieving success. Although the universal rule is supposed to apply equally to all individuals in society, in reality only those from privileged groups have access to the skills and advantages necessary to perform according to it. For example, most four-year universities have three major requirements for admission: (1) a certain grade point average on a set of standard courses taken during high school, (2) graduation from high school, and (3) a set of scores on several standardized tests.

These requirements are applied in the same way whether an individual's last name is Smith or González. However, equal numbers of Smiths and Gonzálezes do not gain admission to institutions of higher education. Apfelbaum argues that although there is a universal rule for admission into a four-year university, in reality individuals of different group memberships have unequal access to the conditions for meeting these requirements. For example, not all high schools have equal numbers of college preparatory classes, the same number of advanced placement classes, equal access to equipment like computers and science laboratories, or adequate textbooks (among many other resources).

The socioeconomic class of the neighborhood where a school is located directly influences available assets. For example, the high school in Palo Alto, California, one of the wealthiest cities in the country, has a very different curriculum than its counterpart in East Palo Alto, a very poor, predominantly African American community. The two high schools, which are only a few miles apart, have different levels of resources that determine whether their students are able to satisfy the college admission requirements.

Table 1 shows that during the 1998–99 school year, schools in the Bay

Area of northern California that had a high percentage of minority enrollment offered fewer advanced placement (AP) classes than schools with predominantly white enrollment. For example, Castlemont High School in Oakland, with 93.5 percent minority enrollment, had no advanced placement courses, while Palo Alto High School, with only 12.7 percent minority enrollment, had 26 advanced placement courses. Obviously, students attending Palo Alto High School had greater opportunities to meet the eligibility requirements for admission to the University of California and other four-year universities than did students attending Castlemont High School. The differential availability of advanced placement courses is not always taken into account when evaluating students during the college admissions process.

The same is true for standardized tests like the SAT (Scholastic Aptitude Test) used for college admissions and the GRE (Graduate Record Examination) used for graduate school admissions. These tests are accessible to anybody who can pay the fee to take them. The knowledge tested in these exams is not equally available to everybody who has completed high school and college, however. In fact, individuals with sufficient economic resources can take expensive training courses designed to improve their scores.[2] So, in effect, there is a universal process by which all individuals regardless of group membership are free to apply to any university of their choice—including prestigious universities like Harvard and Yale—but the skills necessary to gain admission are differentially available according to group membership. At the same time, the dominant ideology is that economic and social privilege is determined through individual merit regardless of group memberships. In fact, most people believe that in the United States everybody is free to choose their profession—be it as a dentist, professor, or plumber. Although all systems of privilege seem equally available, in reality not all professions are integrated, as illustrated in the statistics in topic highlight 16.

As journalist Ray Hartmann notes, statistics are often reported in a way that highlights the absence of **people of Color** in particular professions, rather than a way that underscores the predominance of white men in most professions and in leadership positions. For example, instead of reporting that 93.8 percent of lawyers are white, most publications state that only 6.2 percent of lawyers are people of Color, thus masking the benefits of whiteness (Harris 1993; Hurtado and Stewart 1997).

Table 1 Northern California High Schools and the Availability of Advanced Placement Courses: Fewer Opportunities for Minority Students

Schools with a higher percentage of minority enrollment offer fewer advanced placement classes than schools with predominantly white enrollment. Here are selected Bay Area high schools, showing minority enrollment (excluding Asians) and number of advanced placement (AP) courses offered.

COUNTY	DISTRICT	SCHOOL	ENROLLMENT	PERCENT MINORITY*	AP CLASSES	AP SUBJECTS	AP CLASSES PER 1,000 STUDENTS
Alameda	Oakland Unified	Castlemont	1,786	93.5%	0	0	0
Contra Costa	Acalanes Union	Acalanes	1,328	6.2	16	8	12.0
	Mount Diablo Unified	Ygnacio Valley	1,629	34.0	7	4	4.3
San Francisco	San Francisco Unified	Balboa	1,022	78.9	2	2	1.6
	San Francisco Unified	Lowell	2,527	21.1	31	17	12.3
	San Francisco Unified	Mission	900	71.2	1	1	1.1
San Mateo	Jefferson Union	Jefferson	1,410	93.1	2	2	1.4
	San Mateo Union	Hillsdale	1,279	27.2	11	8	8.6
Santa Clara	Palo Alto Unified	Palo Alto	1,489	12.7	26	8	17.5
	San Jose Unified	San Jose High Academy	977	63.8	0	0	0

*Excluding Asians

Source: ACLU Foundation of Southern California; data for 1998–99 school year

■ Degrouping

Paradoxically, then, the marked collectivity, at the same time that it is becoming an excluded *group* is having its group essence destroyed—that is, it is in the process of being *degrouped*. (Apfelbaum 1979, 198)

A history was denied me / My grandmother's tongue ripped out of my mouth / I was too young to know how to grieve the loss / properly. (Roa 2003)

According to Apfelbaum, any time people are categorized into a group, especially through exclusion, there is a risk of creating a social group identity that will help them unite and fight back. At the same time as individuals are marked into groups—be it by the color of their skin, their ethnicity, their language, or their culture—their *sense* of group belonging has to be destroyed. A positive group identity can facilitate worthy self-perceptions among its members, which may lead to **empowerment.** Therefore, at the same time that subordinate group members are marked, they also have to be **degrouped,** which is accomplished by eradicating their language, culture, and worldview. In essence, dominants take away any tools that would help subordinates develop independent standards and lead them to question the universal rule. However, a dominant group also has to create the semblance of a meritocracy, as opposed to a closed system of privilege. In effect, there has to be a de facto caste system, as illustrated by the statistics in topic highlight 16, at the same time that professional segregation appears to be voluntary and results from individual choice, not group privilege or group oppression. For example, possible explanations for the fact that 98.3 percent of all airplane pilots in the United States are white and male could be that people of Color do not like this profession or that women do not have the manual dexterity to complete pilot training. Similarly, there are several commonly held explanations for the fact that 93.8 percent of all lawyers in the United States are white whereas more than 50 percent of prison inmates are people of Color (Haney and Zimbardo 1998):

1. Individuals have free will to choose whether to be lawyers or criminals, and these statistics are simply the outcome of individual choice.
2. White people are more intelligent than people of Color are.
3. People of Color are biologically predisposed to crime.

Topic Highlight 16. **Blinded by the White: We Caucasians Would Prefer to Ignore Our Preferences**

by Ray Hartmann, *The Riverfront Times,* February 5, 1998

The U.S. Supreme Court, which is 89 percent white, declined Monday to consider a challenge to California's anti-affirmative action Proposition 209. Voters in California, which is 81 percent white, last year passed the measure, which bans "preferential treatment" on the basis of race or gender in state and local government programs. Supporters of the measure praised the justices for letting stand an April ruling by the U.S. Court of Appeals (9th Circuit), which is 89 percent white, which found Proposition 209 was not unconstitutional. "This decision takes California another step closer to achieving a true, color-blind equal-opportunity society," said Gov. Pete Wilson, who, like 100 percent of the nation's governors, is white. Perhaps the most controversial aspect of the proposition is its ban on race-based admission policies in California's state university system, which is overseen by a Board of Regents, which is 82 percent white. As of 1994, an estimated 82 percent of America's resident college students were white, surprisingly low in a country that is 80 percent white, and it is believed that race-based admission policies have kept the number down. Just 16 years earlier, the college population was 87 percent white. At the college-faculty level, where race-conscious programs are also now forbidden by Proposition 209, whites nationally held 86.8 percent of the positions in 1992 (according to the American Association of University Professors). This, too, reflects a drop in white representation because of affirmative-action programs of recent decades. Whites have fared better in other professional categories, however, where the color-blind, equal-opportunity society has not been affected by race-conscious programs:

- Of the nation's airplane pilots, 98.3 percent are white.
- Of the nation's geologists, 95.9 percent are white.
- Of the nation's dentists, 95.6 percent are white.
- Of the nation's authors, 93.9 percent are white.

- Of the nation's lawyers, 93.8 percent are white.

- Of the nation's aerospace engineers, 93.8 percent are white.

- Of the nation's economists, 91.9 percent are white.

- Of the nation's architects, 90.6 percent are white

These statistics were cobbled together from federal Bureau of Labor Statistics information, and they are presented here in a form not normally seen. Customarily, the bureau breaks out only categories such as "female," "black," and "Hispanic," whereas figures for whites are not specified. This is not unlike the reporting of affirmative-action issues, wherein the major newspapers, all of which are primarily owned by whites, and the major TV networks and cable companies, all of which are primarily owned by whites, debate the merits of "preferences" for blacks and women. Even if the subject were, say, the scarcity of black airplane pilots, the experts discussing the numbers and the media reporting them—even those supportive of affirmative action—would come at the subject from the vantage point of how few blacks were pilots. They would never characterize as a "preference" the fact that 98.3 percent of pilots are white. I discussed the twisted perspective about all this with a friend who, like me, is white. She was partly irritated but mainly puzzled: "What's your point?"

Here's my point: We live in a largely white country. The white majority enjoys a disproportionate share of its wealth and comfort and an even greater share of control over most of its institutions. But white power is so pervasive that it's never perceived, or even considered, white power. It's just the way things are. Racial percentages aren't tallied from the white side, only from the "minority" point of view. Thus, when 20 percent of public contracts on a building project are "set aside" for minority contractors, it is a "racial" or "gender-based" issue, but when 100 percent goes to firms owned by white males, it's just, well, reality.

Even many sympathetic to blacks and other people of color will find it quite reasonable that whites have 80-something or 90-something percent dominance of important institutions. After all, the country is 80 percent white, so the statistics are always going to seem racially tilted toward Caucasians, right? Well, not exactly. Only 37 percent of the nation's jail inmates were white in 1994 (as compared with 56 percent in 1978), and only 46 percent of the prisoners executed in the past six decades were white. Only 60 percent of the children living below the poverty line are white. In the same way that numbers can swing disproportionately white, so it is possible for whites to be under-represented statistically. But it never seems to happen when it's a good statistic. Now consider the happy words of Rep. Charles Canady (R-Fla.), a white guy who has authored a federal bill that would eliminate affirmative action at the federal level the way Proposition 209 has in California. Celebrating the Supreme Court's "inaction" on Monday, Canady proclaimed: "The people of California rightly decided to end the divisive race and gender preferences in their state, and it's time for Congress to do the same thing for the whole nation." We're going to end race "preferences" as a nation, eh?

By a "nonracial" vote of the 90 percent white House of Representatives and the 97 percent white Senate, who will then (presumably) have to mount enough "color-blind" votes to override our 42nd consecutive Caucasian president? Yes, we're a color-blind society when it comes to "preferences," all right. We can't see the white. ■

Apfelbaum posits that dominants reinforce the explanation that these statistics are the result of individual choice, not a closed system of privilege, through the use of **tokenism.** That is, a few individuals from the subordinate group are allowed access to privilege. These successful subordinate group members are then used as examples to be followed by members of their group. The fact that not quite 100 percent of all pilots are white (and male) diffuses the argument that there is a caste system that violates the U.S. commitment to democracy. Tokens are proof that a meritocracy exists. However, tokens are not completely accepted by dominants. Psychologically strong and secure tokens risk the development of standards of achievement that are independent of the universal rule. Furthermore, tokens could facilitate other subordinate group members' success. By their very position, therefore, tokens are constantly watched by dominants. Their status is scrutinized for any flaws, and if any are found, they are judged more harshly than those of similarly situated dominant group members. For example, a woman professor in an engineering school where

99 percent of the professors are white and male is more likely to be harshly evaluated by her colleagues and by her students. She is subject to internalizing these negative judgments and beginning to doubt her abilities. Tokens serve the dominant group's needs but rarely are in a position to exert influence to change the existing intergroup power differential or to help develop a different standard of achievement. A recent study of faculty at the prestigious Massachusetts Institute of Technology (MIT) showed that few women faculty at that institution felt fully accepted by male faculty (see topic highlight 17). In addition to not receiving equal pay and resources for their research, they also felt marginalized in subtle and not so subtle ways, including these examples:

1. Women faculty were excluded from major decisions in their departments.
2. In the MIT Engineering Department, women faculty were rarely on faculty search committees.
3. During faculty search committees, women faculty were asked to talk only to women job candidates, not to male job candidates.

All of these situations made many MIT women faculty feel that they were not as valued as the men faculty, accelerating the degrouping process.

The internalization of the dominant standard happens very early in life. By age five, most children are aware of the fact that males are evaluated as superior to females. By the time they are nine, they are aware that being brown or black is not as good as being white. Awareness of class differences takes longer—mostly because the majority of neighborhoods are segregated by class (Steinhorn and Diggs-Brown 2000) and because in the United States class is not as salient a category as race or gender. Topic highlight 18 summarizes ethnic and racial identity development in children using a comedy segment from Whoopi Goldberg's one-woman Broadway show. In this sketch, Goldberg plays a seven-year-old African American girl who drapes a white blouse over her head to pretend she is blonde. She has learned from television and other sources that living a glamorous life entails being blonde. Her mother's admonishments against self-deprecation have little effect on her because of the counterevidence around her.

Whoopi's character believes that being blonde and blue-eyed will give her access to white privilege. After all, her toys, like Ken, Skipper, and Malibu Barbie, and television shows like "Love Boat" all indicate that

Topic Highlight 17. **New Study at MIT Finds That Female Faculty Members Still Feel Marginalized**

by Scott Smallwood, *Chronicle of Higher Education,* **March 20, 2002**

Female professors at the Massachusetts Institute of Technology, even when paid about the same as their male colleagues, often feel like second-class members of the faculty, according to a new study. The information came in a series of reports released this week on the status of women throughout the institution. The reports follow up on the well-known 1999 study on female professors in MIT's School of Science, which showed that women were being paid less and given fewer resources than men. That report, in addition to leading to change at MIT, prompted similar studies at numerous other universities. The new reports, put together by four separate faculty committees, repeatedly point to women's complaints about being marginalized.

In a letter to the faculty about the new studies, Provost Robert A. Brown wrote that gender bias takes various forms, including salary inequities, but also "more subtle forms of marginalization." He cited women who feel excluded from major decisions made within their own departments. "The overall result is the same," he wrote. "Women faculty members are not equal participants in our faculty community. A comment is repeated over and over that MIT is a 'man's world.' This must change." Nancy H. Hopkins, a biology professor who spurred MIT to examine gender discrimination in the sciences, said that more than 200 professors came to a faculty meeting Monday to discuss the new reports. She said she was optimistic that MIT's willingness to confront the issue would prompt other institutions to do the same. But Ms. Hopkins said the marginalization of women would be hard to undo. "You can fix salaries," she said. "But how do you change this? Each incident may be tiny, but when they accumulate they add up to a lot. It's a consciousness issue."

Some examples of the discrepancies highlighted in the reports:

- From 1990 to 1998, the Electrical-Engineering and Computer-Science Department hired 28 men and no women.

- In 2000, 14 percent of the Ph.D.s awarded in the field at MIT, the University of California at Berkeley, and Stanford University—the three institutions where the department gets most of its new faculty members—went to women.

- In another engineering department at MIT, women are rarely on faculty search committees. A female professor said that during faculty searches, she was asked to talk with a candidate only if that person was a woman.

- In the School of Architecture, one female professor said faculty searches can be tainted by gender bias: "You have a mediocre guy and a woman. When they talk about the guy, they talk about his degrees. When they talk about the woman, they say she hesitates when she speaks, that she's too heavy, that she won't fit."

The study in the Sloan School of Management featured in-depth interviews, including meetings with all six tenured female professors in the school. The researchers "found a big difference particularly between the feelings of access, empowerment, and belonging of the men and the women faculty. None of the men had a fully negative experience on these dimensions; only one woman had a clearly positive experience." ∎

whiteness will give her economic security and an "exciting" life. Whoopi's character is so convinced of this that she is willing to sit in a "vat of Clorox" and wear a shirt over her head to be white and blonde. Apfelbaum would argue that this little girl has internalized the dominant group's standards, inculcated through the media, and that even the toys available to her contribute to the degrouping process.

Yet, as powerful as the three mechanisms are, Apfelbaum and other researchers have outlined several interventions by which these negative views of self can be reconstituted through group empowerment.

Social psychologists are deeply aware of the consequences of having stigmatized social identities. The deleterious effects of not having one's ethnicity and race affirmed are especially difficult for children. An excellent example is provided in Whoopi Goldberg's one-woman show, which ran on Broadway a few years ago. In it, Whoopi portrays a seven-year-old African American girl wearing a white shirt over her head, which she pretends is her "long, luxurious blonde hair." She asks the audience "Ain't it pretty?" seeking their approval.

The young girl proceeds to show the audience how the shirt on her head moves like long blonde hair by swinging it back and forth and pretending it gets into her eyes. The little girl then tells the audience that her mother told her that her "long, luxurious blonde hair" was nothing but a shirt. The little girl gets upset and tells her mom that she's going to have not only "blonde hair and blue eyes" but that she's also "going to be white" because she saw on television that you could go "to the optometrist office, and he has blue eyes in his desk drawer." The little girl associates being white with having "a dream house, and a dream car, and dream candy, and a dream horse and me and Barbie are going to live together with Ken and Skipper and Malibu Barbie."

The little girl tells her mother "I don't want to be Black no more," because all she sees her mother do is "work and work and not have an exciting life," unlike the lives of people she sees on television. Furthermore, the little girl tells her mother that "she don't even look like nobody on TV, not even on the 'Justice League,' not even on the 'Smurfs.'" Her mother replies that "even if you sit in a vat of Clorox till hell freezes over you ain't gonna be nothing but Black." The little girl had already tried it, and concluded her mother "was right because I sat in the Clorox and I got burned. And she said I just have to be happy with what I got, but look see (she removes the shirt from her head and reveals her black hair)—it don't do nothing." The little girl dislikes her hair because "it don't blow in the wind, and it don't cascade down my back. It don't, and I put that bounce and behaving stuff in it, and it didn't even listen."

In a dramatic turn, the little girl turns to the Broadway audience and suddenly notices that many audience members have hair like hers. She asks one audience member whether her hair "is just naturally like that [curly]? I guess nobody look like you on TV either, huh?" The little girl turns toward the audience and starts pointing to all of the different people and says, "And she got it and he got it, and nobody got no shirt on [their head]. And nobody on TV look like none of you all." Then the little girl poignantly asks, "Well, who do those people [on television] look like, huh? Maybe if I am lucky, I don't have to wear no shirt on my head; then, maybe, if I'm lucky, I will grow up to be cute." ■

■ Regrouping through Empowerment

There are many ways of speaking out. . . . The (group) must undergo a positive reevaluating of the peculiarities and the specific characteristics . . . served as marking criteria for exclusion by the dominant group . . . the (group) must rediscover its own cultural roots and historical background. (Apfelbaum 1979)

Their words, now mine, woven into a / tempestuous cloth that's wrapped protectively / around my shoulders / Their words, now mine, used to reclaim my / history / to reclaim what was taken from me. (Roa 2003)

The field of psychology proposes individual-level solutions to combating oppression and stigma. As a society most people do not believe privilege is largely determined by group membership. As Apfelbaum states,

there exists here a basic underlying value conflict which gets triggered by our forays into questions of domination, and which in turn deeply threatens to shake up the currently held world view. How can one reconcile, on the one hand, the realities of power-based social relations along with all their related practices of discrimination/exclusion with, on the other hand, the claim that we all belong to a truly democratic society, which enforces the principle of a universal humanity and "which institutes a fundamental law for all and affirms the equal rights for *individuals* based on the unity of mankind." (Varikas 1997, 9; Apfelbaum 1999, 304)

Therefore many are also skeptical that group membership alone is used to impose oppression and to derogate people's social identities. They see the solution to overcoming group-based stigma as being to foster individual self-esteem. For example, the main psychological intervention advocated for children of Color who feel bad about their racial characteristics like their hair or their skin color, as Whoopi Goldberg's seven-year-old character does in topic highlight 18, is to bolster their self-esteem. Self-esteem is an intervention addressing a person's individual identity not their social identity. The stigma placed on a particular social identity has very little to do with the individual as a person. Racism, sexism, and homophobia are based on stereotypes not on in-depth information about an individual *as a person*. Individual-level interventions, although certainly helpful, deny the social nature of how individuals build their social identities. Changes in social conditions of oppression are not going to come about solely through individual improvement, but rather through individual improvement coupled with collective action. Several writers propose that a positive self-identity as well as social identity occur through interventions that connect personal validation *and* group empowerment.

The work of Lorraine Gutiérrez and her colleagues is an important example of social and **personal identity** interventions that lead to empowerment. Gutiérrez (1990) defines empowerment as "the process of increasing personal, interpersonal, or political power so that individuals can take action to improve their life situations. Empowerment theory and practice have roots in community organization methods, adult education techniques, feminist theory, and political psychology" (149).

Gutiérrez's definition of empowerment recognizes the link between individual and group empowerment and how the increase in a group's power can enhance the functioning of its individual members. Gutiérrez's work is aligned with the social psychological concept of an individual's life space. Furthermore, this definition of empowerment assumes that all individuals have social identities that confer either privilege or stigma, depending on the groups to which they belong. The process of empowerment occurs at both the individual and group levels. Four psychological changes are crucial in moving an individual from apathy or despair to empowerment: increasing self-efficacy, developing group consciousness, reducing self-blame, and assuming personal responsibility for change.

Increasing Self-Efficacy

The social psychologist Albert Bandura was the first to propose the beneficial aspects of increasing **self-efficacy,** which he defines as "beliefs in one's capabilities to organize and execute the courses of action required to produce given attainments" (1997, 3). Individuals who feel self-efficacy are also likely to perceive several courses of action for solving a given problem, to increase their efforts in given endeavors, to have resiliency in the face of adverse conditions, and to experience less stress and depression in the face of failure.

Self-efficacy at the group level is manifested in empowerment. Group empowerment leads to its members' restitution of self. Erika Apfelbaum (1999) further elaborates how degrouped groups can restitute their group identities by shifting their frame of reference from the dominant group to their own group's norms. As an example, in the last part of the Whoopi Goldberg sketch, her character notices that other Black people with hair like hers are not wearing white shirts over their heads. She also notices that people in the audience don't look like the people on television. In fact, people in the audience look like her, and they don't seem ashamed or as if they want to change themselves to appear more white or like characters on the "Love Boat." So she shifts her basis of comparison from whiteness to the diversity exhibited in the audience. In other words, the group in the audience allows her to shift to a different group norm that empowers her to take the shirt off and be proud of her hair. By shifting from the dominant group's "universal rule" of what is desirable—blonde hair—to the "nongroup's" norm of curly, dark hair, she begins to see herself and others like her in a new and more favorable light. The audience as a group empowered Whoopi's character in ways that the mother's individual affirmation alone could not. It took her family's affirmation *and* the audience's self-acceptance of their group characteristics to give her the courage to remove the white shirt from her head.

Developing Group Consciousness

Developing group **consciousness** involves an awareness of how political structures affect individual and group experiences. Henri Tajfel calls this process a perception of **cognitive alternatives** to the existing power disparity between groups, and Patricia Gurin and her colleagues (1994) call it **consciousness.**

Reducing Self-Blame

Through reducing self-blame, members of subordinate groups come to recognize the stigma of their identity as residing not in their innate biological makeup or solely in them as individuals. Instead, they are able to see their circumstances as an outcome of both what they do and of the restrictions placed on them by society.

Assuming Personal Responsibility for Change

Taking personal responsibility for change counteracts some of the potentially negative results of reducing self-blame. In assuming personal responsibility, individuals see themselves not as victims of the system that oppresses them, but as full human beings capable of agency within those restrictions. They recognize that individuals are not *just* an accumulation of their stigmatized social identities, but also have self-identities that are the same as those of other human beings who may have more privileged social identities. For example, the characters in Michelle Serros's poems (reprinted in the last chapter) are two women who are not well educated, are overweight, and do not meet mainstream standards of beauty, yet they still have agency and are capable of being witty, funny, warm, thoughtful, intelligent, complex, and having other worthwhile characteristics.

The process of assuming personal responsibility is similar to Paolo Friere's (1973) notion of becoming a subject (or an active participant in society) rather than remaining a powerless object. The four psychological changes that lead to empowerment are not hierarchically arranged stages, but rather they should ideally happen simultaneously. Individual interventions to build individuals' self-esteem will be much more powerful if they also include the other three aspects of empowerment.

Gutiérrez's research focuses on social work settings but can be applied to many other areas as well. According to Gutiérrez (1990), empowerment must take place within the context of a "helping relationship" that is nonhierarchical in nature. Experts telling the client or subordinate person what to do will not lead to empowerment. Instead, a helping relationship entails collaboration based on equality. Second, interventions should include the individual, the family, and the community. In other words, effective interventions should take place in the individual's life space, not simply within the individual. Gutiérrez also proposes several characteristics that these interventions should have:

- accepting the person's definition of the problem,
- identifying and building upon existing strengths,
- engaging in a power analysis of the client's situation,
- teaching specific skills, and
- mobilizing resources and advocating for clients.

These interventions are aimed at building an individual's sense of self-efficacy and restitution of self. If done properly, they help the client feel a sense of agency, which is not often given to poor people or people with stigmatized social identities.

Reclamaciones: Toward a Whole Self

In the poem by Jessica Roa entitled "Reclamation" (see topic highlight 19) she restitutes her sense of self, at both the individual and social identity levels. She reclaims her history, the language "torn from her," and her cultural heritage. After she accomplishes all this, she is ready to take charge of her life. Next, we discuss several ways each of these reclamations can take place.

Reclamation of Ethnic Labeling through History

By 1848 Mexico had lost approximately 50 percent of its territory. . . . With the signing of the Treaty of Guadalupe Hidalgo, the Mexican American people were created *as a people:* Mexican by birth, language and culture; United States citizens by the might of arms. (Alvarez 1973, 924)

A primary basis for group formation is that group members have the right to name themselves. If a dominant group refuses to accept a subordinate group's self-labeling, or worse, if dominants are the only ones with the power to name, subordinate groups find themselves in disarray. Subordinate groups have spent much of the twentieth century fighting for the right to name themselves accurately. Rodolfo Alvarez (1973) in his classic article "The Psycho-Historical and Socioeconomic Development of the Chicano Community in the United States" traces the different cohorts of Mexican descendents in the United States and the labels they have forged in efforts

Topic Highlight 19. "Reclamation"

by Jessica Roa (2003)

A history was denied me
   My grandmother's tongue ripped out of my mouth
   I was too young to know how to grieve the loss
     properly

     the wound healed
     in the shape of my Americanness

   "Work hard and you'll succeed," I heard
   And so I did

   My 22nd year the truth was revealed to me
     "White man is on top"
   "And you? Sorry, honey, you're somewhere near
     the bottom"

   Anger
   Anger turned my insides into a seething crimson

   The death of my ignorance shook me hard and
     choked me out of my complacency
   I have fallen many times since the first breaths of
     truth were inhaled

     But I always come back to standing
   And now
   A language has been found
   The language of the colonizer twisted
   and shape-shifted
   to resist
   to empower

   Their words, now mine, woven into a
     tempestuous cloth that's wrapped protectively

around my shoulders
Their words, now mine, used to reclaim my
   history
      to reclaim what was taken from me

And to make the promise
   to speak the words
That this is only the beginning ■

to name themselves. He identifies four specific cohorts: the Creation Generation (1849–1900), the Migrant Generation (c. 1901–1942), the Mexican American Generation (c. 1943–1966), and the Chicano Generation (c. 1967–1973).[3] He defines *generation* as "a critical number of persons, in a broad but delimited age group, [who] had more or less the same constraints imposed by a dominant United States society. Each generation reflects a different state of collective consciousness concerning its relationship to the larger society; psycho-historical differences related to, if not induced by, the economic system" (920).

The Creation Generation (1849–1900)

Alvarez identifies the Creation Generation as those Mexican descendents living in the southwestern territory annexed by the United States after the Mexican-American War, which officially ended in 1848 with the Treaty of Guadalupe Hidalgo. Former Mexican nationals became U.S. citizens overnight but lost many of their civil rights as well as their land ownership. They became "colonized" on their own land and were labeled and treated as "minorities." The Creation Generation labeled themselves primarily as Mexican because of their national origin and regionally as Tejanos, Manitos, Californianos (Mexican American Texans, New Mexicans, Californians), and so on.

The Migrant Generation (1901–1942)

By the turn of the century, the U.S. population was becoming increasingly urbanized and required large farms to produce food. As such, there was a need for a cheap labor pool and the United States looked to Mexico to provide "immigrant" labor. Large numbers of Mexicans crossed the largely un-patrolled

U.S.–Mexican border to work in the agricultural fields. Even though legally they were considered immigrants, Alvarez (1973) argues that these individuals are more accurately considered migrants for four major reasons:

1. Mexican nationals crossing the border were not coming into a "fresh social situation where they were meeting the host society for the first time" (927). They did not arrive with the "'freedom to define themselves" to have "one's self-image and self-esteem determined almost exclusively from one's presentation-of-self" (927). Instead they left a "lower *class* status in Mexico to enter a lower *caste* status in the United States without being aware of it" (928). In other words, "their experience upon entering the United States was predefined by the well established social position of pre-1900 Mexican Americans as a conquered people (politically, socially, culturally, economically, and in every other respect)" (927–28).

2. Mexicans migrants were coming to a land that was virtually the same as the land they were leaving—language, cultural practices, and even geographical terrain did not change dramatically as they traveled from their homeland to the southwestern United States.

3. The "border" they crossed was in many areas nothing more than an imaginary line because at the time it was not policed, or even clearly marked. Also, many times crossing the border entailed simply wading across a river, walking across a path, or crossing a bridge—acts that were so short in time and effort that there was no "anticipatory socialization," unlike the situation of European immigrants, who traveled as long as two weeks before arriving to U.S. shores (Alvarez 1973, 929).

4. The ease of crossing the border with little official documentation further contributed to Mexicans not being fully aware that they were entering another country. Unlike, say, Irish immigrants, who had to apply, be accepted, and sign official documents, all of which required a *conscious* choice to leave one national identity behind and accept a new one, Mexicans simply took a seven-minute walk across a bridge or river and entered a terrain that looked pretty much the same as the one they left. They were often joining extended family members and obtaining jobs similar to the ones in their home country. Such a migration hardly entailed a deep commitment to change, modify, or reflect on their identity.

The Migrant Generation further reinforced the Creation Generation's **identification** as "Mexican," preventing them from slowly becoming "American." In addition, the economic caste status to which most Mexicans were confined created additional ties of solidarity between longtime residents of the Southwest and the more recent Mexican arrivals. Cultural and language ties were revitalized, and the population grew, as many of these migrants established permanent homes in the United States.

The Mexican American Generation (1943–1966)

The Mexican American Generation emerged around the time of World War II and was characterized by a growing loyalty to the United States. According to Alvarez (1973) young people of this generation asked their parents:

> What did Mexico ever do for you? You were poor and unwanted there. Your exodus reduced the unemployment rate and welfare problems that powerful economic elements in Mexico would have to contend with, so they were happy to see you leave. You remained culturally loyal to the memory of Mexico, and you had dreams of returning to spend your dollars there. You sent money back to your family relations who remained in Mexico. . . . And what did Mexico do for you except help labor contractors and unscrupulous southwestern officials to further exploit you? I am an "American" who happens to be of Mexican descent. I am going to participate fully in this society because, like descendents of people from so many other lands, I was born here, and my country will guarantee me all the rights and protections of a free and loyal citizen. (931–32)

Alvarez (1973) asserts that the Mexican American Generation shifted their loyalty from Mexico to the United States because of a focus on their economic and educational success *in comparison* to their parents' generation. Had they compared themselves to white Americans, they would have seen how much they lacked. During this time, Mexican Americans moved to follow the jobs available in industrial centers outside the Southwest, most notably in Chicago. Significant numbers of Mexican Americans joined the military during World War II. Both of these factors increased this generation's view that indeed they were making progress in this country. This generation's shift from a caste system—where individuals had little or no education, were mostly employed in agricultural work, and had no avenue for social mobility—to a lower-class status in which individuals obtained some degree of education, employment in industrial jobs, and participation in the military, all led to the birth of the Chicano Generation.

The Chicano Generation (1967–1973)

The Chicano Generation shifted their focus from comparing themselves against their parents' generation to comparing themselves against other U.S. citizens:

> So you are a loyal "American," willing to die for your country in the last three or four wars; what did your country ever do for you? If you are such an American, how come your country gives you less education even than other disadvantaged minorities, permits you only low status occupations, allows you to become a disproportionately large part of casualties in war, and socially rejects you from the prestigious circles? As for me, I am a Chicano, I am rooted in this land, I am the creation of a unique psycho-historical experience. I trace part of my identity to Mexican culture and part to United States culture, but most importantly my identity is tied up with those contested lands called Aztlán! My most valid claim to existential reality is not the false pride and unrequited loyalty of either the Migrant Generation or the Mexican American Generation. Rather, I trace my beginnings to the original contest over the lands of Aztlán, to the more valid psycho-historical experience of the Creation Generation. I have a right to intermarriage if it suits me, to economic achievement at all societal levels, and to my own measure of political self-determination within this society. I have a unique psycho-historical experience that I have the right to know about and to cultivate as part of my distinctive heritage. (Alvarez 1973, 940)

The Chicano Generation realized that although they were legal citizens of this country, they did not have the same rights and privileges as whites. Their parents' small economic success gave them the space to begin to question U.S. society and their place within it. In addition, during the 1960s many traditional racist and sexist ideologies were under attack. Different ethnic and racial groups challenged the conventional views of "racial" inferiority and provided alternative frameworks to honor their language and culture; the women's movement was also part of the mix. At the same time, immigration from Mexico had slowed down, and the United States was experiencing economic stability and growth. The Chicano Generation had higher aspirations than any of the previous generations, and they mobilized politically to force the U.S. government to respond. During this time many affirmative action programs were developed to recruit Chicanos/as to higher education, financial aid was established to help them with the expenses, and Chicano Studies programs flourished in several universities. It was a time of major social upheaval and social change. The ethnic label *Chicano/a* came to signify an allegiance with the demands voiced as part of the **Chicano Movement,** whose proponents explicitly rejected an immigrant/foreigner status. Those who identified themselves as Chicanos/as claimed their rights as U.S. citizens without rejecting their Mexican heritage and language.

Multiplicity in Current Ethnic Labeling

Mexican descendants' complex, collective U.S.–based history through the mid-1970s has produced multiple constructions of ethnicity that are available for the later generations to use as they create their own social identities (Hurtado, Gurin, and Peng 1994). These culturally defined and generationally specific identities provide *multiple* models that members of the later generations can use in thinking about their own identities. Across time, people of Mexican descent developed many ways of dealing with ethnicity. While particular generations developed prototypic conceptions of what it means to be an American of Mexican descent, the new identities did not replace older ones. New ways of thinking about ethnicity were added while older ways were refined and retained. Thus, each successive generation had a richer cultural repertoire of identity constructions to draw upon. Multiplicity of ethnic labeling is the cultural and historical legacy of U.S. Mexican descendants.

Henri Tajfel, Erika Apfelbaum, and others recognize the importance of having sovereignty to name one's group. Chicanos/as have fought for this right by creating the field of Chicano Studies and by giving young people the opportunity to think about how they wish to name themselves. The twentieth century was about subordinate groups' struggles to obtain the right to name themselves—African Americans, feminists, Asian Americans, Chicanos/as, and **Latinos/as.** The twenty-first century will be about how best to represent the hybridity of the Chicano experience to encompass groups of Latinos/as who are not from Mexico, but have joined Mexican Americans' political and social struggles in the United States.

As a result of this complex history, people of Mexican and Latin American descent residing in the United States have many ethnic identification labels available to them. Some labels, like Mexican, Nicaraguan, and Salvadoran, refer to a specific country of origin and are most commonly, although by no means exclusively, used by recent immigrants. Others—such as Tejano/a, Manito/a, and Californiano/a—refer tò U.S. geographical origins and highlight regional identities and cultural practices. Other labels refer to different views on cultural **assimilation** and are inherently political. Ethnic labeling is therefore another way to demonstrate an individual's **identification** and consciousness; examples are *Chicano/a* for Mexican descendants and *Boricua* for Puerto Ricans. Both terms highlight ethnic cultural pride and the hybridity of cultural and language practices in these U.S. communities. Other labels, like Latino/a and Hispanic, demonstrate the necessity of expressing cultural and political solidarity that encompasses different national groups. However, it is worth mentioning that *Latino/a* is more often viewed as a politically progressive pan-ethnic label than is the term *Hispanic,* which many feel originated in the U.S. government rather than emerging organically from any of the different U.S. Latino/a communities (Moya 2002, 42). The label *Hispanic* is also viewed by many as emphasizing the European ancestry of Latin Americans while ignoring their indigenous and African roots.

Reacting to the politically constructed rather than historically based origins of *Hispanic,* poet Elba Sánchez (2003) highlights the fact that "hisss panicsss" have no geographical referent (see topic highlight 20): "hisss panicsss/as in from Hissspania?/where's that?" She claims that the purpose of using the label Hispanic is for the dominant group to avoid learning about the complexity and diversity of the Latino/a population. Instead of understanding the historical basis for the diversity in ethnic labeling as well as the different geographical, linguistic, and different national origins, "*el patrón*" (the boss) needs "to homogenize / *a toda la gente*" (all the people). According to Sánchez, homogenizing all Latinos/as into "Hispanics" is an effort to make them more acceptable: "hisss panicsss/does it make me/more acceptable?/hisss panicsss/the ultimate white wash."

Columnists Patrisia Gonzales and Roberto Rodriguez echo Elba Sánchez in their tongue-in-cheek column written for April Fool's Day on why the label Hispanic should be eliminated from the U.S. census (see topic highlight 21). Nonetheless, the label Hispanic has great currency on the East Coast and more recently in Texas, whereas *Latino/a* is more commonly used on the West Coast and is appropriated by those who directly oppose the use of *Hispanic.*

Following Spanish language conventions, gender is indicated in many of these ethnic labels by the ending vowel—labels ending in *a* refer to a female whereas those ending in *o* indicate a male. For example, Latin*o* refers to a male of Latin American descent, and Latin*a* refers to a female. As is common in English, the generic is male so when referring to the group the male pronoun is traditionally used—Latin*os*. In an effort to avoid sexism in the language, many writers use Latin*os/as* or vice versa Latin*as/os*. Most individuals in the United States who have origins in Latin America use multiple labels, depending on the social context and according to their own particular historical and immigration experiences (Hurtado and Arce 1987).

Reclamation of Language

And now
A language has been found
The language of the colonizer twisted
and shape-shifted
to resist
to empower
. . .
And to make the promise
to speak the words
That this is only the beginning

(Roa 2003)

As part of the Americanization policies instituted by the U.S. government during the first half of the twentieth century to assimilate immigrants, Chicano/a children were punished in schools for speaking Spanish (García and Hurtado 1995). As late as 1968, the Civil Rights Commission found widespread civil rights violations by school officials who often punished Chicano/a students in the Southwest for speaking Spanish on the school premises. The punishment ranged from verbally chastising them to physically punishing them. Even though there was great public outrage at this kind of treatment, fifteen years later students in south Texas reported similar kinds of treatment for speaking Spanish. Although many of the schools did not have written rules against speaking Spanish, a substantial number of students reported being detained after school, being made to run laps, or even having their mouths taped if they spoke Spanish on school premises (Hurtado and Rodríguez 1989).

Topic Highlight 20. "Hiss Panics"

by Elba Sánchez (2003)

hisss panicsss
your panic
   her panic
their panic
   our panic
whose panic
   HISSS panic

so much raza
el patrón panicsss
he's in a tizzy
all this brown
makes him sooo dizzy
he needs to homogenize
a toda la gente

hisss panicsss
as in from Hissspania?
where's that?
non-existent country
non-existent people
no history or geography
no tongue to speak
of struggle
hisss panicsss
does it make me
more acceptable?
hisss panicsss
the ultimate white wash
it's hisss panic
to erase un MOVIMIENTO

hisss panicsss
  with lots of mayo
  in a big patty melt
  y hasta con guaca moe lee
  hisss panicsss
  mcpanicsss
  coorspanicsss

  chale! not me!
  no way!
  that ain't mine baby
  I continue to be
  Sí, yo sigo siendo
  simplemente
  pura RAZA ■

More recently the passing of English-only legislation, the outlawing of bilingual education, and even the abolishment of affirmative action have created a situation where the maintenance of Spanish becomes a counter-hegemonic reclamation of self. Chicano/a scholars have written eloquently about the loss of their native *lengua* (language) and the shame of those who retained it. The reclaiming and recuperation of Spanish becomes a way to restitute their sense of self.

Usually the repression of Spanish occurred in schools, as narrated by historian Emma Pérez (1991, 174):

Like many *tejanas/os* who attended Anglo schools through grade school, I too was punished for speaking my parents' tongue on playgrounds and classrooms. Spanish set my brother and me apart. Anglo teachers peered at us when we spoke Spanish, the way white women peer at me now when they try to interfere in a circle of Chicanas speaking together in Spanglish, reaffirming our **mestizaje.** As a child in Anglo schools, I realized quickly that I had to learn English, to pronounce it accurately, precisely. I was ridiculed for my accent, I was pushed into dark closets, disciplined for calling a student *gringo* [a derogative term for a white American male]. I practiced at night, staring up at the ceiling in my bedroom, reciting the alphabet. In English. Forgetting *la lengua de mi gente* [the language of my people]. Not knowing that the loss of language is loss of memory.

Topic Highlight 21. I.N.S. Disbands, Census Eliminates "Hispanic" Category

by Patrisia Gonzales and Roberto Rodriguez (2002)

President W. Bush is set to issue an executive order on March 31 that will disband the Immigration and Naturalization Service (INS). In issuing the executive order and making the announcement on César Chávez's birthday, President W. Bush will cite the historical mistreatment of Mexican people as the cause. "As my good friend César used to say, '*Ya Pasta!*' " On the same day, the U.S. Census Bureau will itself issue a controversial directive that henceforth eliminates the "Hispanic" category. Due to the major recent embarrassment regarding the INS approval of visas for two dead al-Qaida operatives, the first announcement was widely anticipated, whereas the census directive has taken many bureaucrats by surprise. The census decision was reached as part of an out-of-court settlement with the Mexican American Lawyers in Defense of Freedom (MALDEF). The human-rights organization filed a class-action lawsuit (*Rodriguez X v. U.S. Census Bureau*) in 1979, challenging the accuracy and appropriateness of the category. Rodriguez X initially petitioned the bureau—on the basis of his primarily indigenous ancestry—to allow him to be excluded from the Hispanic category. In denying his request, the bureau stated: "While not challenging the indigenous character of the plaintiff, the new category includes Mexican Americans, which is intended to better count people of Spanish ancestry." In filing the class-action lawsuit, Rodriguez X charged: "As someone of Mexican origin—whose indigenous heritage is rooted on this continent for thousands of years—I have nothing to do with 'Hispania.' "

In 1986 and 1989, the lawsuit was amended to include Central Americans and Puerto Ricans, respectively. Canek (Charlie) Bonampak, a bureau official, admitted that his agency had come close to accepting the Rodriguez X petition, but worried that other Mexican Americans might follow suit. "Without Mexican Americans, there is no Hispanic category," said Charlie, noting that they constitute two-thirds of all those classified as Hispanic. "When Central Americans and then Puerto Ricans joined the lawsuit, we already knew that there was not a single group within that category that preferred Hispanic as a primary form of identification. We did, however, find a small group in Northern New Mexico and Southern Colorado that preferred 'Hispano,' but even they rejected the Hispanic designation. Frankly, we pressed on because that was the institutional mode we were in. Elimination of that category would have meant a lot of unemployed bureaucrats," admitted Charlie. "By the 1990s, we also knew that the Hispanic category had become a Frankensteinian nightmare, primarily because even we were treating it as a legal and scientific category, which it isn't. We had created a category of some 30 million people that had begun to define the other 270 million. Of course, Hispanic is not a racial category either. But as a result of our ineptness, we created the nonsensical 'non-Hispanic white' term, which caused bureaucrats to assume that most Hispanics are white. In fact, the opposite is true. It became so confusing that even we were confused. My own children, Maya and Balam, were being classified as 'non-Anglo, non-Hispanic Mayans.' So we were convinced, but we couldn't agree upon an alternative." One plan included placing Mexican Americans, Central and South Americans (a la 1930) into their own indigenous category. Tom Ridge, director of Homeland Security, suggested color codes (black, brown, yellow, white, and rainbow) in place of racial categories. However, Attorney General John Ashcroft objected, insisting that Arabs might slide into the brown category undetected, though he denied that his opposition constituted racial profiling. "All the options create bureaucratic nightmares," said Charlie. "We began in 2000 by creating a group called 'Latin American Indians,' and while somewhat helpful, it didn't address the Rodriguez X petition. After 23 years, this mess created nothing but panic for us—his-panics, her-panics, high-spanics, hic-spanics, house-panics, and even mouse-panics. In the end, it does still sound like 'spics.'" "As of *April 1*, rather than accept the Rodriguez X petition, we will be eliminating the governmental Hispanic category altogether," said Charlie. "There's no substitute. People will be free to choose whatever identity they want." Co-plaintiff Olga González, who gave birth to her child, Citlamina, recently in Denver, noted that hospital officials tried to classify her child as Hispanic and white. When she informed them that they were from the Mexican Otomi nation, the hospital refused to count her as indigenous and instead left her birth certificate blank. "It's indicative of what this country thinks of us," said González. ■

Chicanos/as reclaim Spanish as a public acknowledgment of the linguistic limbo many experience as they are socialized in Spanish at home, then confront language repression when they enter school (Hurtado and Rodríguez 1989). Learning the "colonizer's language" was a traumatic event for many Chicanos/as and one that deeply influenced their thinking about the meaning of having their own "lengua" and about its relationship to social identity.

Chicano/a scholars are quick to point out that just as their cultural, historical, and political existence is a mixture of their experiences as Mexicanos, Americanos, and Indígenas [Indians], their language, too, is a mixture. The U.S.–Mexico border has become a metaphor for Chicanos'/as' racial, cultural, national, and linguistic hybridity. As Sonia Saldívar-Hull (2000, 173) explains,

I invite readers not fluent in Spanish to experience a sense of life on the border as we switch from English to Spanish. Sometimes we translate, at other times we assume the nonnative speaker will understand from the context. Many Chicanas/os speak only English. Reading Chicana texts puts several demands on the reader, including the expectation that the reader will be knowledgeable in multiple Chicana and Chicano linguistic, cultural, and historical contexts. While most contemporary Chicana writers and critics have been formally educated in the United States and are fluent in English and Spanish, many of the writers code-switch between the two languages.

Having access to multiple discourses in two languages—from formal English to Spanglish to Caló—provides insight into the political nature of how intellectual "merit" is defined. Many Chicana/o scholars who came from working-class backgrounds experienced the derogation of their parents by schools and other institutions because their parents did not speak English. Emma Pérez relates her confrontation with language differences when she started school in Texas:

When I entered the first grade, I cried each day after school. I lay my head on my mother's lap, a woman who was denied the right to read and write the language of the colonizer in a land that belonged to her ancestors. She brushed my hair back, comforting me. I couldn't articulate what I say so easily now. I couldn't say that the woman who comforted me, the woman who held power, beauty, and strength in my eyes, that Anglos dismissed her because she couldn't fill out their damn forms. I couldn't say that the school was infested with white students, so alien to me. And that day the white teacher shoved me against a wall because I didn't recite the "Pledge of Allegiance." I didn't know it. But I knew "El Rancho Grande." (Pérez 1991, 177–78)

The use of Spanish by Chicana/o and Latino/a scholars in intellectual production becomes a political assertion of the value of their heritage and the means to create a sense of identity directly tied to a Chicana/o and Latino/a experience (see topic highlight 22).

Reclamation of Cultural Practice through Art and Performance

Art is about healing. When people participate in art, when they make it, when they view it, it is the same as making yourself well (Amalia Mesa-Bains, quoted in Portillo and Muñoz 1990).

Until very recently, most schools did not have a multicultural curriculum designed to educate racial and ethnic groups about each other's histories, languages, and cultures. Most of the focus in schools has revolved around studying race differences between whites and African Americans, excluding other ethnic and racial groups.

This void in the school curriculum has increased the importance of Chicano/a artists in creating awareness about Chicano/a culture, history, and language. Many of them have made cultural practices central to their artistic production, making those inside and outside their communities aware of the beauty of Chicano/a culture. Singer Lila Downs, for example, performs classical *boleros* (romantic ballads) as well as folk songs from Oaxaca (see topic highlight 23).

Downs chose this genre of music to honor her Mixtec mother. Most recently, she is "coming closer to the land of her father, the United States" (Meléndez 2002, 1E). Lila Downs concludes that her artistic explorations

Topic Highlight 22. Chicanas/os' and Latinos/as' Views on the Importance of the Spanish Language for Their Identity

"So, if you want to really hurt me, talk badly about my language. Ethnic identity is twin skin to linguistic identity—I am my language. Until I can take pride in my language, I cannot take pride in myself." (Gloria Anzaldúa, quoted in Fiol-Matta, 2001, 152)

"Returning to *la mujer* [the feminine] scares me, re-learning Spanish scares me. . . . In returning to the love of my race, I must return to the fact that not only has the mother been taken from me, but her tongue, her mothertongue. I want the language, feel my tongue rise to the occasion of feeling at home, in common. I know this language in my bones . . . and then it escapes me. . . . 'You don't belong. *¡Quítate* [get out]!' " (Cherríe Moraga, quoted in Fiol-Matta, 2001, 152)

"The border-crosser develops two or more voices. . . . We develop different speaking selves that speak different aspects of our identity." (Guillermo Gómez-Peña, quoted in Fiol-Matta, 2001, 150)

"Theorizing colonialism as abuse can yield insight into why we may feel that no matter how much we modify our actions and attempt to measure up to norms imposed from the outside, we do not seem able to develop satisfactory strategies to protect the self. No matter how well we speak English, or how light or dark our skin is, or how well we do in our school work, there is always the lingering doubt that we are not 'loved for who we really are' but for the facsimile of the dominant culture that we can, with varying success, represent. Perhaps the key to the colonized child's survival can be found in Albert Memmi's assertion that 'the colonized's liberation must be carried out through a recovery of self and of autonomous dignity' " (Liza Fiol-Matta 2001, 151). ■

allowed her to discover her roots: " 'I was reborn when I realized who I was, what my essence is. That's when I began to learn the history of our peoples, the history of the world' " (8E).

Chicano/a artists have been central in rescuing Chicano/a cultural practice as inspiration for their art. For example, the "Chicano Art: Resistance and Affirmation" (CARA) exhibition in 1990 was the first major exhibition of Chicano/a artists, and it had an impressive national and international impact. Many working-class Chicanos/as had never seen themselves reflected in art production nor visited a museum before the CARA exhibition arrived in their cities. As Alicia Gaspar de Alba (1998) describes, museum curators were surprised at the long lines of people waiting in the Texas heat to enter the CARA exhibition when it came to El Paso.

> "Chicano exhibit draws 4,000 on first day," reads a headline in the *El Paso Herald Post*. . . . The *El Paso Times* relates that, "For the first time in the museum's 32-year history, guards asked people to wait for the crowds in the galleries to thin out." Some visitors waited up to fifty minutes in the August heat, distracted from their thirst by the Ballet Folklórico and the mariachis that had been commissioned to entertain the audience and by the lowriders parked alongside the museum, on display as local examples of Chicano art "on wheels." (Gaspar de Alba 1998, 219)

The content of the CARA exhibition spoke profoundly to many Chicanos/as across the country, who were happy finally to see themselves, their culture, their history, and their communities reflected in art. Art images portrayed the daily life of Chicano/a neighborhoods, as in the case of painter Carmen Lomas Garza (see figures 12 and 13), who depicted such activities as a family making tamales and a neighborhood *posada* (Christmas celebration reenacting Joseph and Mary's search for an inn in Bethlehem). Depictions also communicated a history that has been systematically ignored in U.S. schools; one example was Yreina D. Cervántez's painting *Homenaje a Frida Kahlo* (Homage to Frida Kahlo; see figure 14).

For many, viewing the image of Frida Kahlo led to educating themselves about this woman's triumphs over physical illness, her international prominence in the art world, and her marriage to Diego Rivera, another iconic figure in Mexican art. Art communicates with and educates viewers at multiple levels. The more viewers see themselves in art, the more they learn about themselves and their origins as a people. As a viewer at the

Topic Highlight 23. Conflicts of Two Cultures Alter Mexican-American Singer's Ego

by Claudia S. Meléndez

In her music, Mexican-American singer Lila Downs captures the struggles of migrants who come to the United States in search of opportunity. But her sweet and powerful voice slides this bitter tale of hardship easily into the souls of listeners.

Downs . . . began this musical journey on her first CD, "La Sandunga," in 1997. She performed classical boleros and famous folk songs from Oaxaca, Mexico, the land of her mother, with a distinct hint of jazz. Her next CD, "Yutu Tata," explored Zapotec and Mixtec songs.

Her latest production, "Border," continues her voyage. She's coming closer to the land of her father, the United States, with songs that describe the migrant worker experience. She dedicated "The Border" ("La Linea") to "the Mexican migrants, to the spirits of those who have died crossing the line."

Trained as a classical musician, an opera and jazz singer, Downs stretches her voice, bringing it as low as the workers stooped on strawberry fields and as high as the hawks watching over them.

With a unique blend of jazzy Mexican folk music, she incorporates elements of her indigenous roots into her melodies: the high-pitched voice, the drums made of turtle shell, the rain stick, all combined in the contemporary arrangements of Downs and her husband and musical partner, Paul Cohen.

Born in Mexico of Mixtec mother and American father, Downs, 34, spent her youth between Minnesota and Oaxaca and says she experienced discrimination in both countries. As a young woman, the classism and racism entrenched in Mexico pushed her away from her mother's culture.

 Shock of Ethnicity

"I felt like just another North American," she says, switching effortlessly between English and Spanish. "When I realized I was racially, culturally different, first I went into shock. All of us in Mexico, those of us who are **mestizo,** feel that insecurity about our roots."

But at the University of Minnesota, where she studied music and anthropology, she said she found an environment that made her confront her own prejudices. At first, this identity crisis made her quit school and eventually pushed her to find herself.

"I was reborn when I realized who I was, what my essence is. That's when I began to learn the history of our peoples, the history of the world," she says.

Her 1999 CD "Yutu Tata" ("Tree of Life") is rich with an exploration of her mother's culture. Based on ancient codices narrating the stories of the indigenous people of Mexico, the 13 songs in Mixtec, Zapotec, Nahuatl, and Spanish pay homage to those roots she once rejected. Some penned by her, they describe the reverence for the elements, animals, the cycle of life and death, and her own life story, as in "Stone Seed."

"I'm the daughter of a man of stone / a deer and wind gave birth to me / I was born the color of the earth from a fire and steam bath."

With songs such as "The Failed Bracero," "The Girl," and "Transit," Downs focuses "Border" on the immigrant experience, a phenomenon she said she began witnessing when she was young among her relatives who, unlike her, had no means to cross the border legally.

"I used to listen to the stories of my countrymen who used to come to the border when I was little, but I didn't know what to do with those stories, until now," she said.

■ A Sacred Side

Downs has dazzled many audiences, from the jazz patrons who frequent the El Sol y la Luna bar in Mexico City where she performs, to Bay Area fans who flock to her performances whenever she returns. She believes her music has resonated with people who are in search of a kind of music that is more spiritual, more soulful.

"I've found a very sacred side to my singing. At concerts, people come to tell me they're touched, and it makes me feel that I was born to do this, to touch people. That makes me happy." ■

■ 12. *Tamalada* (Making Tamales), 1987, gouche, 20 x 27 inches, by Carmen Lomas Garza, collection of Don Ramon's Restaurant, San Francisco, California

Albuquerque Museum of Art wrote in the comment book after seeing the CARA exhibition: "Finally, we [Chicanos/as] can see our culture, not only on the outside, but on display [inside] where others can learn and appreciate who we are today and why" (Gaspar de Alba 1998, 222).

Chicano/a artists also exalted what is now called a *rasquache aesthetic,* which is described as "subverting the dichotomies between 'high' and popular culture" and affirming artistic production coming from Chicano/a working-class communities (Gaspar de Alba 1998, 10). Practices that were often characterized as "exotic" and as producing "low-class" art—like velvet paintings, "gaudy" folklórico costumes, and "simple" mariachi music— were rediscovered as sources of inspiration and beauty. In essence, *rasquachismo* is the notion that Chicano/a working-class people can create objects of beauty in spite of poverty and lack of education. Building altars for **El Día de los Muertos,** enjoying *norteño* music, learning the words to

■ 13. *Posada* (Inn), 1987, gouche, 20 x 28 inches, by Carmen Lomas Garza, collection of Marina D. Alvarado and Gilbert Mercado Jr., Los Angeles, California

corridos (ballads retelling actual events), and many other cultural expressions from working-class Chicano/a communities are no longer considered "low culture." Instead, Chicano/a artists highlight the complexity of the aesthetic and the value of this cultural production for the restitution of self and as a means to avert what has been variously called in the social sciences self-hatred, internalized racism, and marginality.

■ Regrouping the Degrouped Group

Thus, the process of **regrouping** is the affirmation of the historical and functional existence of the (group). (Apfelbaum 1979, 203)

Erika Apfelbaum (1979) writes that degrouped groups need to reclaim their history, language, and culture to feel the strength and beauty of their group membership. Until the subordinate group can escape from the grip of

■ 14. *Homenaje a Frida Kahlo,* by Yreina D. Cervántez

the universal rule and create their own standards of achievement, they cannot escape their status as a nongroup. An essential part of the reacquisition of self is to transform previous negative characteristics as positive affirmations of self. "Mexican," "Chicano/a," "Pocho," "Spanglish," "Tex-Mex," "rasquache"—all have to be appropriated and embraced as sources of strength and pride. Thereby, the subordinate group can then step out of its (degrouped) status and finally occupy its space in society as a legitimate group "as it steps out of the parentheses of subordination" (Apfelbaum 1979, 203).

■ Summary

In this chapter we reviewed the role of group life in creating and maintaining personal and social identity. Following are the major points of the chapter:

- Individuals exist within groups that either facilitate or hamper them from developing different aspects of their sense of self. That is, identity is not only an individual characteristic, but is fostered and maintained through participation in group life.

- The organization of groups in society will influence how individuals relate to each other and the development of their sense of self.

- French social psychologist Erika Apfelbaum proposes that Western democracies are based on the notion of *meritocracy* where all individuals, regardless of group membership, have access to society's privileges if they meet universal standards of performance.

- Standards of performance are enforced through a *universal rule* that is said to apply to all individuals regardless of group membership. In fact, those individuals belonging to privileged groups have greater access to the resources necessary to meet the standards set forth in the universal rule.

- Erika Apfelbaum proposes a third mechanism of intergroup control: degrouping. That is, individuals are grouped into subordinate groups *at the same time* as they are denied any positive rewards for belonging to the group. The degrouping process is accomplished by taking away any positive characteristics of the group, such as its language, culture, and values, to avoid in-group solidarity. Degrouping is further reinforced through the promotion of a small number of subordinate group members to function as *tokens,* thereby defusing the accusation that *all* subordinate group members are denied access to privilege.

- Regrouping of the degrouped group can be accomplished by interventions that connect personal validation and group empowerment. *Group empowerment* can be accomplished by subordinate group members acquiring or enhancing their group's language, history, and culture.

In the next chapter we propose some conclusions and examine new social identities in the making. As the United States becomes more ethnically and racially diverse, and as Latinos/as become a larger proportion of the U.S. population, scholars are developing new and exciting ways of understanding the formation of social identities.

■ Discussion Exercises

1. Identify different student organizations on your campus.

2. With a small number of students, discuss what each of these organizations contributes to students' sense of identity and belonging to different communities.

3. Have each student in your group interview a couple of participants in some of these organizations, asking them their motives for joining, how their membership contributes to their sense of identity and belonging, and how their lives would be different if they didn't belong to these organizations. Add as many other questions as your group finds interesting and worth pursuing.

4. Return to your group, share the findings from your interviews, discuss your own memberships in different organizations, and answer for yourselves the same questions you asked other students.

■ Notes

1. Erika Apfelbaum argues that subordinate groups may in fact be "nongroups" because they are hampered in providing their group members with the positive aspects of belonging to a group. Therefore, the "subordinated group becomes . . . a group in parenthesis," indicating that in many ways the subordinated group is a "nongroup" (1979, 198–99).

2. Katherine Cohen, a private college admissions counselor based in New York City, charges as much as $28,995 for her platinum package, which involves reviewing a student's applications, brainstorming essay ideas, holding mock interviews, and helping to plan course loads and college visits (Cohen 2002). Obviously, only students with substantial financial resources can hire Cohen or another of the 4,000 private admissions counselors now practicing across the United States.

3. Alvarez (1973) does not give exact dates for each of these generations, with the exception of the Creation Generation. Otherwise he gives major events like "during World War II" or "during the Vietnam War" as markers for these generations. We provide years to simplify the discussion.

Conclusions

The Future of Identity Formations

Some places the border is a muddy river, too thin to plow, too thick to drink. Other places it's just a line in the sand. Over the years mapmakers redrew it, wars moved it, nature yanked it all around as the course of the Rio Grande shifted. But what would it take to make it disappear altogether? (Gibbs 2001, 38)

A recent *Time* magazine article announced the disappearance of the U.S.–Mexico border and renamed both countries "Amexica" (Gibbs 2001; see figure 15). Perhaps this pronouncement is a bit premature, but there is no doubt that globalization patterns are increasing, paralleled by increasing **transnationalism** between the United States and Mexico. These changes have enormous consequences for new identity formations and for cultural transformations. As recently as 1960, **Latino/a** immigrants were relatively scarce; less than 20 percent of Latinos/as were foreign born. By 1980, however, 37 percent of Latinos/as were foreign born, with increasing numbers of immigrants from all parts of Mexico and other countries of Latin America. Since 1980, immigration from Latin America has continued at a rapid pace. The 2000 census shows that immigrants make up the majority of the adult population in California, the nation's most populous state. Furthermore, the majority of immigrants are Latinos/as and the majority of immigrant Latinos/as are of Mexican descent. Mexican immigrants are characterized by their extensive contact with their communities of origin through family visits, phone calls, and promotion of immigration to members of their extended family. This is a situation quite different from the one experienced by European immigrants at the turn of the last century, when an ocean and unreliable modes of communication often meant cutting all ties with their native countries for at least a generation or two (Alvarez 1973). Extensive and frequent contact with Mexico means that immigrants sustain their language and

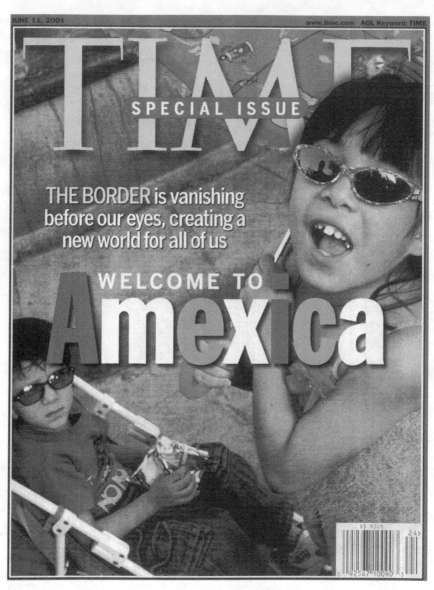

■ 15. *Time* magazine cover for the "Amexica" special issue

cultural vitality, incorporating cultural changes that occur in their country of origin, thus renewing and updating their cultural repertoires even after immigrating. This situation is less likely to lead to complete **assimilation** (Gurin, Hurtado, and Peng 1994).

Coupled with the drastic changes in the composition of the U.S. Latino/a population is the unprecedented population growth among Latinos/as. Population changes have occurred throughout the United States, but most strikingly in California, the most multicultural state and the one where the majority of Latinos/as reside. In 1940 Latinos/as were indeed a minority constituting only 6 percent of the state's population, or approximately 374,000 residents. By 1980, the Latino/a population had reached 4 million and by 1990 had nearly doubled to more than 7 million. By 2000, nearly one-third of the state's residents were Latino/a. In fact, one of the significant findings of the last U.S. census was the surprising growth in the Latino/a population, as a recent *Time* magazine article notes:

> The biggest political news of the 2000 Census was that Hispanics—more than half of them tracing their roots to Mexico—have become the largest minority group in the United States, surpassing African Americans at least six years sooner than expected. Where that's happening is turning out to be as surprising as how fast. Of the congressional districts that saw the biggest increases in their Latino populations over the past decade, not a single one is in a state along the Mexican border. Rural areas saw huge growth in Hispanic populations, but so did cities and suburbs. By the end of this year, four of the eight largest U.S. cities may have Hispanic mayors. "It's the only part of the electorate that is growing," says Antonio Gonzalez, president of the Southwest Voter Registration Education Project. (Tumulty 2001, 74)

The 1998 elections were the beginning of Latinos/as flexing their electoral muscle. A few of the milestones in this election included these:

1. In California, a grandson of Mexican immigrants became the first Latino in 120 years elected to statewide office when Cruz Bustamante won the race for lieutenant governor ("Parties divide up" 1998).
2. Democrat Loretta Sánchez, a thirty-eight-year-old Latina, beat Republican U.S. Representative Robert Dornan, a former nine-term congressman, to represent Orange County, one of California's most conservative districts ("State Democrats retain edge" 1998).
3. In Colorado, Democrat Ken Salazar won the race for attorney general and was the first Latino elected to statewide office in that state's 125-year history (Chronis 1998).

In spite of their potential to affect electoral politics through their numbers and their considerable gains, as these facts illustrate, Latinos/as are still in transition from considering themselves a minority to proactively engaging in mainstream politics. As a recent *Time* magazine article noted, "Though the Latino and African-American populations in the United States are roughly the same size, 6 million more blacks are registered to vote. Turnout rates are lower than average even among more educated and affluent Hispanics" (Tumulty 2001, 74). An additional challenge is to get Latino/a immigrants to become naturalized citizens in order to exercise their voting rights.

■ Multiple Social Adaptations to Cultural Transformations

The increasing number of Latinos/as, most of whom are immigrants, has implications for their cultural adaptations and their social and ethnic **iden-tifications.** These changes influence how willing an ethnic or racial group is to relinquish its ethnic distinctiveness. Unlike the situation at the turn of the century, when the dominant ideology was to make all ethnic groups into non–ethnically distinct Americans, contemporary ethnic and racial groups do not necessarily perceive their ethnicity as a barrier to their social and economic integration (Hurtado, Rodríguez, Gurin, and Beals 1993). The current social and historical context in the United States favors multiculturalism. Even though the issue is highly contested, the vibrant debate encourages many ethnic group members (with a substantial number of whites agreeing) to believe that cultural maintenance should not be a detriment to economic and social advancement (Phinney 1996).

Historically, the main concepts used in the social sciences to understand multiple social group identities have been culture conflict, self-hate, marginal man, internalized oppression, oppositional identity, and assimilation, to name a few. These negative views of self have existed and indeed continue to exist to some extent, but what remained undocumented was the other side of the coin—that individuals can also survive and, in fact, thrive under existing power disparities. The political movements of the 1960s provided the aperture for a broader participation of different groups in creating knowledge (Goldberger et al. 1996). Those individuals that were theorized about, written about, and objectified are "talking back," to quote bell hooks (1989), thus expanding who, what, and for what purpose knowledge is constructed (Crenshaw 1993; Harris 1990). Scholars like Gloria Anzaldúa, Cherríe Moraga, Chela Sandoval, and Patricia Williams, among others, propose that multiple group identifications can be potential avenues for dismantling previous prejudices and unfair practices. In effect, progressive scholarship as well as the integration of academia have helped to reconceptualize previously problematic **social identities** as a source of strength and a diversification of mainstream culture. As previously silenced and stigmatized groups speak out through academic production and political mobilization, the value of certain social identities is being reconfigured.

The normal distribution, presented in figure 16, provides a useful conceptual tool for illustrating what has been excluded in the study of group differences. Historically, the emphasis in assimilation and **acculturation** research has focused on the left tail of the bell curve—that is, it has focused on identifications that are not particularly healthy, ones for which the only solutions are to assimilate to the dominant mainstream or spend a lifetime of psychological and social alienation. Progressive scholars have reacted to this tradition by emphasizing the right tail of the normal distribution of successful adaptations to cultural transformations *in spite of* the costs involved in rejecting assimilation (some writers argue that indeed there is a much higher cost to assimilation than to remaining an outlier; see, e.g., Cuádraz 1996; Rendón 1992). The ability to successfully negotiate multiple group memberships has been called mestiza consciousness (Anzaldúa 1990), differential consciousness (Sandoval 1991), or a state of concientización (Castillo 1995). The uncharted territory is in the middle. We have ignored the "spread of diversity" (Gould 1996); that is, how large numbers of individuals deal with multiple group identifications and how this variety of adaptations is related to psychological outcomes.

The distribution of these identifications has changed through the process of history and the change in demographics, as illustrated in figure 17. As multiculturalism has become more acceptable in our society, **people of Color** are less likely to see their ethnicity and race as a source of stigma. The cultural adaptation encompassed in the concept of marginal man is less likely to happen in the 2000s than it was in the 1950s, when complete assimilation was perceived as the only normal adaptation to cultural transformation. Also, as mentioned earlier, the fact that people of Color are rapidly becoming the majority of residents in many states also increases their numbers in various occupations and professions. This augmentation provides a critical mass that helps individuals circumvent feeling marginalized, at least within specific social contexts (Cuádraz and Pierce 1994;

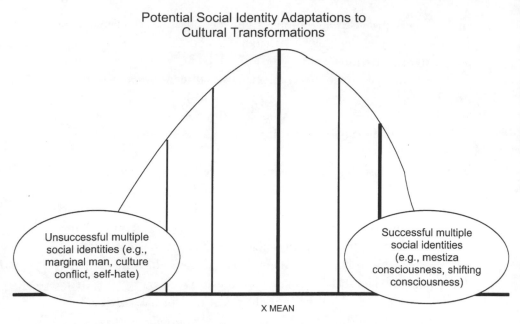

Potential Social Identity Adaptations to
Cultural Transformations

Unsuccessful multiple
social identities (e.g.,
marginal man, culture
conflict, self-hate)

Successful multiple
social identities
(e.g., mestiza
consciousness, shifting
consciousness)

X MEAN

16. Negative versus positive cultural adaptations distributed along a normal curve

Rendón 1992). As these changes occur for different groups, we can expect
the normal distribution of cultural and social adaptations to widen so as to
include greater, not fewer, responses to cultural transformation. To be sure,
we will still have the marginal man among us, but there will be more
movement of the distribution toward the right tail, increasing the number
and diversity of positive cultural adaptations.

New Developments in the Study of
Social Identities: Transnationalism
and Transculturalism

The change in countries of origin and the increasing numbers of Lati-
nos/as has had dramatic consequences for social identification. As emphasized in the previous chapters, Chicanos/as have always been a diverse
population in terms of their social identifications. Even though there are
many overarching similarities between different groups of Chicanas/os,
there is also a lot of internal diversity according to the region individuals

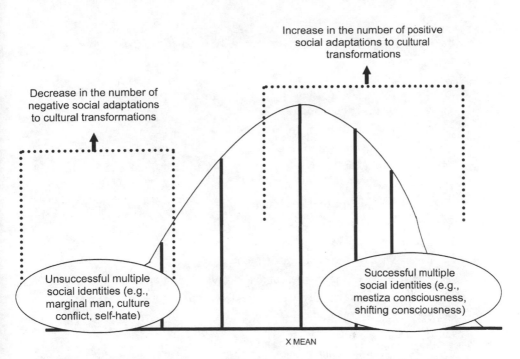

Increase in the number of positive social adaptations to cultural transformations

Decrease in the number of negative social adaptations to cultural transformations

Unsuccessful multiple social identities (e.g., marginal man, culture conflict, self-hate)

Successful multiple social identities (e.g., mestiza consciousness, shifting consciousness)

X MEAN

■ 17. The relative increase in positive, and decrease in negative, cultural adaptations

grew up in (e.g., Texas, California, Chicago, etc.), the number of generations resident in the United States (first, second, or third generation and beyond), degree of intermarriage, language skills in English and Spanish, and levels of education. In addition, ethnic self-labeling changes for Mexican descendants throughout their lives. The way people think of themselves in their teenage years is different from how they think of themselves as they grow older and have more diverse experiences. Higher education has a powerful influence on students' identity transformations. Many Chicana/o students are the first generation in their families to attend institutions of higher education, which may lead them to question aspects of their identity they had previously taken for granted. For example, a Chicana who grew up in a working-class neighborhood may be very aware of the effects of poverty and privilege, and of how her ethnicity affects her in the world. However, she may never have questioned her views on Catholicism because everybody in her family and her neighborhood was Catholic. During college she may come in contact for the first time with peers who are neither Catholic nor even religious. Through the process of **social**

Topic Highlight 24. "How Latino/a Are You?" Quiz

You know you are truly Latino/a . . .

1. If you have ever been hit by a chancla.
2. If you grew up scared by something called "El Cucui."
3. If others tell you to stop screaming when you are really just talking.
4. If you light a candle to the Virgin Mary on the night of the Lotto drawing.
5. If you use your lips to point something out.
6. If you constantly refer to cereal as "con fleys."
7. If your mother yells at the top of her lungs to call you for dinner, even if you're in a one-bedroom apartment.
8. If you can dance merengue, cumbia, or salsa without music.
9. If you use "manteca" instead of olive oil and can't figure out why your butt is getting bigger.
10. If you call your sneakers "tenis."
11. If you have at least thirty cousins, not including loco Julio working at Don Pipo's.
12. If you can't imagine anyone not liking spicy food.
13. If you are in a five-passenger car with seven people in it and a person shouting "subanse, todavia caben" [Get in! You can still fit!].
14. If whenever you feel under the weather, you compulsively dab some "vapor rub" all over your chest and inside your nostrils.
15. Your mom packs your "lonchera" every day, even though you've just turned thirty-two.
16. If you have your country's flag hanging over your rearview mirror.
17. If you just don't get tired of the so-called "sopitas."
18. If you have a bottle of Tapatio in your purse.
19. If your favorite heroes were "El Chapulin Colorado," or "Cantinflas."
20. If you don't need any explanation for more than three items. ■

comparison, she is forced to think about the role of religion in her life and about how those beliefs may determine who she is and what values she holds, especially around issues of premarital sex and abortion—issues that remained unexamined until she entered college. Thus, a great deal of identity transformation takes place for most students between their first year in college and the time they graduate.

In spite of all these differences, Chicanos/as also have some overarching historical, cultural, and language similarities that have allowed them to participate in a distinctly Mexican culture. With the growing number of non-Mexican Latinos/as, cultural diversity has increased, although the Latino/a population can still relate on many cultural and language issues. Furthermore, many Latino/a immigrants to the United States come from working-class backgrounds and seek greater economic opportunities, another commonality across cultures. Others come as a result of their political activism and subsequent persecution in their countries of origin. Regardless of their country of origin, Latino/a students in our classes still chuckle as they rate themselves on the scale of "How Latino Are You?" (see topic highlight 24) recalling how their family life and neighborhoods were distinctly different from the education they receive at the university.

Transnational Identities

At the same time as there is an increasing acceptance of cultural diversity in this country, the world as a whole is coming closer together through mass communication systems and rapid travel. Globalization along with greater cultural diversity in the United States have made Chicanos/as aware of their transnational ties to Mexico and the rest of Latin America. In addition, Chicanos/as are moving to all areas of the United States, leaving behind their traditional population concentrations in the Southwest and the border region (see figure 18).

María Hinojosa, a prominent Chicana journalist, relates the transculturation she experienced, from considering herself specifically Mexicana to feeling a connection with other Latinos/as as well, when she moved in 1979 from Chicago to New York to attend college:

New York taught me that culturally I was more than a Mexicana. There were Puerto Ricans and Dominicans on my street; I went to school with them, along with Cubans, Argentines, and Peruvians; I bumped into Salvadoran and Chilean refugees in community centers. I began to see that I

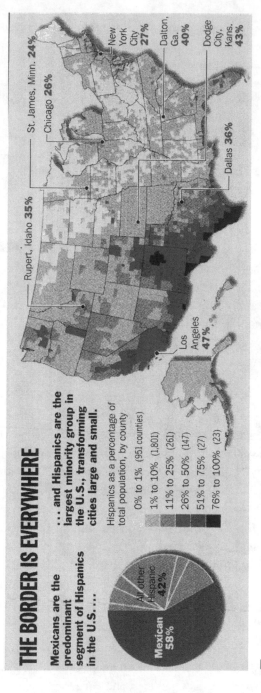

THE BORDER IS EVERYWHERE

Mexicans are the predominant segment of Hispanics in the U.S. . . .

. . . and Hispanics are the largest minority group in the U.S., transforming cities large and small.

Hispanics as a percentage of total population, by county

0% to 1% (951 counties)
1% to 10% (1,801)
11% to 25% (261)
26% to 50% (147)
51% to 75% (27)
76% to 100% (23)

All other Hispanic **42%**

Mexican **58%**

St. James, Minn. **24%**
Chicago **26%**
New York City **27%**
Dalton, Ga. **40%**
Dodge City, Kans. **43%**
Dallas **36%**
Rupert, Idaho **35%**
Los Angeles **47%**

18. "The Border Is Everywhere," a map showing the geographic distribution of the U.S. Latino/a population

was part of a continent—from Patagonia to el Caribe. I still called myself a Mexicana, but I came to consider myself something bigger, a Latina without borders. (Hinojosa 2001, 79)

The increasing numbers of non-Mexican Latinos/as results in an increase in intermarriage rates among different Latino/a groups. Sociologists López and Espíritu (1990) predict a Latino pan-ethnicity in the not-so-distant future, resulting from a true commingling of various Latino/a cultures, rather than from a false homogenization created by the U.S. government labeling (see chapter 3). María Hinojosa eventually married a Dominican artist and sees her two children juggle their multiple identifications as they grow up in New York City far from the U.S.–Mexican border:

In 1996 my son was born. Raúl Ariel Jesús de Todos los Santos Perez-Hinojosa, we joked he would be the first Domini-Mex New Yorker. . . . My son will face different challenges than I did—just as he has different advantages. There will always be something of a border between him and his paisanos [countrymen]—as real as the border between him and his best friend Bruke, whose parents are political refugees from Eritrea; or between him and his classmate Attiya, whose mother is a corrections officer in the Rikers Island jail and whose dad was shot to death in his livery cab. Or the border between him and his blond friend Lily, who loves to come to our house to eat tacos and dance merengue but who lives in an apartment three times the size of ours on posh West End Avenue. While his heritage may be the same as mine, his crossings will be different. Ideally, I hope my kids can be Latinos without borders. (Hinojosa 2001, 79)

However, even those who do not intermarry begin to feel like "Latinos without borders." The increased facility of transportation between the United States and Mexico, as well as the NAFTA (North American Free Trade Agreement)[1] regulations of the 1990s make it easier for Chicanos/as to go back to their parents' hometowns in Mexico. As a result, they are able to create a **transnational identity** based on actual experience rather than simply an ideological commitment to maintaining Mexican culture. The experience of Rebecca Hernández, profiled in topic highlight 25, is illustrative. What becomes apparent from Rebecca Hernández's border crossings is that ethnic socialization and social identification take place within larger units than nuclear families—encompassing aunts, uncles, neighborhoods,

Topic Highlight 25. Two Hometowns/Bay Area's Second-Generation Mexican Immigrants Advance While Keeping One Foot in the World of Their Parents

by Louis Freedberg

When Rebecca Hernandez visits the tiny Mexican village her mother left 30 years ago, she knows her way around almost as well as she knows her home in Union City. Born in the United States 29 years ago, she is the first member of her extended family of Mexican immigrants to graduate from college—Berkeley and Harvard, no less—and she has worked as a budget analyst in New York.

Yet when she returns to Tlacuitapa—a place in which she never lived—she visits with relatives, runs into old friends, and stops by her godmother's house on Tlacuitapa's mostly deserted streets.

"I like the small-town atmosphere," she says. "It is safe. It is a cohesive community. People greet each other on the street."

Rebecca is not alone among second-generation Mexican immigrants. Their experiences suggest that the trajectory of U.S.–born children of Mexican immigrants will be radically different from those of other immigrant groups.

In those groups, experts say, ties to their parents' ancestral homes dissipate rapidly. But because of Mexico's geographic proximity, Mexican immigrants have been able to refresh and reinforce their ties to their old country.

Ruben Rumbaut, a sociologist at UC Irvine, says that scholars and policymakers have focused too much on first-generation immigrants, and not enough on their U.S.–born children. What happens to them will determine what happens to the immigrant group, and their long-term influence on U.S. society.

Experts say the ties of the youthful generation to their Mexican roots could shape the speed at which the Mexican immigrants and their descendants become assimilated into the mainstream of the United States.

"Will [it] be a long, slow, economic mobility, like Italians,' where it takes years to move up the social ladder?" asked Michael Fix, director of immigration studies at the Urban Institute in Washington, D.C. "Or will it be the Chinese model, where it takes one generation to move rather rapidly into the middle class?"

Rebecca, now an administrator of a San Mateo County reading program, has been to Tlacuitapa at least a dozen times, sometimes for months at a time.

 ## Forging a New Bond

Yet her connection to Mexico is profoundly different from the direct ties of her parents and grandparents. The older generation would send money in the form of remittances to relatives back home, build and maintain houses in their home villages, or even leave open the option of retiring to Mexico. They have true "transnational" identities.

Not so with Rebecca and the younger generation, most of whom have no intention of living in Mexico. Instead, their ties are based on nostalgia, staying in touch with the dwindling number of relatives in the old country, and often the sheer habit of repeated visits.

Rebecca has been going to Tlacuitapa—a rural village so tiny it doesn't appear on any official road map—since she was 1. Because her parents had legal papers, it was as easy as climbing into the station wagon and taking a leisurely four-day drive to get there.

Whether ties like Rebecca's will be sustained over time, and into the next generation, remains to be seen. Already the pressures of work, family life, and the costs of traveling to Mexico mean they travel less and less frequently to Tlacuitapa.

"In the long term there is a very powerful shift toward increasing rootedness and embeddedness in the American experience," said Marcelo Suárez-Orozco, a Harvard anthropologist. "It is only for a small number of second-generation kids [that] their primary references will be their country of origin."

But for now, the children of Mexican immigrants from Tlacuitapa and elsewhere have been able to resist some of the potent acculturating forces of U.S. society. In part that's because of the conscious efforts of their parents and grandparents to re-create many aspects of the lives they left behind in Mexico.

■ A Culture Based on Family

Hundreds, if not thousands, of descendants of former Tlacuitapa residents live in or around Union City. Many get together almost weekly in Kennedy Park, especially during the summer, to celebrate birthdays, baptisms, graduations, and other events. Many attend the same church, Our Lady of the Rosary.

The U.S.–born children of Mexican immigrants have an unusually close relationship with their parents. Many of them live with their parents well into their 20s, some even after they have gotten married.

Perhaps the key factor in binding them together is that almost all the children born here speak Spanish with an astonishing fluency. Most do so proudly.

Blanca Amezquita Hernández, Rebecca's mother, is a member of the sprawling Amezquita clan. Artemio Amezquita, the family patriarch, died six years ago. The matriarch, Rosa, lives with Blanca and other family members in a townhouse in Union City. Seven out of eight of Rosa's children live in the United States. Three of her sons—Rebecca's uncles— live within blocks of each other.

Rosa still maintains a huge house in Tlacuitapa. The beds in each of the two-story house's 10 bedrooms are made up year-round, in silent anticipation of the family's return.

As the family's unofficial historian, Rebecca has drawn up a family tree, which includes 200 of her relatives. Her regular trips to Tlacuitapa, she says, have helped her stay in touch with her roots.

■ Strong Male Ties

The attachments to Tlacuitapa are especially strong among the male children. Jorge Amezquita, 23, whose father, Cruz, first came to Union City in 1967, has gone back every year since he was 16. He even met his Tlacuitapan-born wife at the annual fiesta there two years ago.

"I just couldn't imagine marrying someone who wasn't from there," said Amezquita, who works at the Dreyer's ice cream factory in Union City.

Ironically, immigrant children must contend with dual messages they receive from their elders. Parents want their children to maintain close ties to their homeland, but they also want to spare them bitter days of trying to survive in a remote, drought-stricken place like Tlacuitapa, as well as their days as farmworkers in the agricultural lands on which Union City was built.

Becoming a part of the United States—working here, marrying here, having children here—is the only way forward. In an unexpected way, visits to Tlacuitapa help reinforce the U.S. identity of the U.S.–born generation.

"In those towns, there is nothing," Rebecca said. "If my parents hadn't moved here, I would be stuck in one of those towns." ■

communities—increasing the likelihood of transnational identification as many families move from Mexico to the United States and visit relatives often. Bilingual exposure and interaction with various socialization norms make the self more cognitively complex and transnational.

Transculturation

In the original definition of acculturation proposed by anthropologists Redfield, Linton, and Herskovits in the 1930s was the notion that when different ethnic groups come in contact, the culture of both groups may be affected by their interactions. They declared that acculturation "comprehends those phenomena which result when groups of individuals having different cultures come into continuous first-hand contact, with subsequent changes in the original cultural patterns of either or both groups" (Redfield, Linton, and Herskovits 1936, 61). Given the increases in the number of people of Color in the United States and in economic globalization, unidirectional acculturation is not as feasible as it was even in the recent past. **Transculturation**—that is the process of functioning, at some level, in the social life of a different cultural group than your own—is more likely to happen on the U.S.–Mexican border than in other areas of the United States. Transculturation is promoted by the many U.S. manufacturers relocating to Mexico to take advantage of the abundance of low-cost labor. While most workers in these companies are Mexican, many of the managers are imported from the United States, creating what has been called the "NAFTA Man":

NAFTA Man is not only bilingual, he's also bicultural. He speaks Spanish on the factory floor in Mexico but yells in English at his kids' T-ball games. He knows when to bribe in Mexico (to a traffic cop) and when not to (during an environmental inspection). He prefers chiles rellenos to pot roast, gets his allergy medicine in Mexico but his MRI in the United States. He has a two-sided wallet for pesos and dollars and would practically kill for a cell phone that works in both countries. "Well don't you know who we are," laughs John Castany, president of the Reynosa Maquiladora Association, which has 110 mostly gringo members. "We're schizo. Border culture is just, well, different." (Thomas 2001, 53)

Although NAFTA Men (there are few women managers) are supposedly "genetically engineered by the new border economy" it is not solely out of economic necessity that dominant group members are becoming trans-culturated. The discourse of multiculturalism has created spaces that allow them to begin constructing transculturated identities. Ironically, the attacks on affirmative action have resulted in a vibrant area of research in higher education focusing on the benefits of cultural diversity for *white* students rather than on claims of social justice for students of Color. Social psychologist Patricia Gurin served as the expert witness on behalf of the University of Michigan in the court cases over their affirmative action policies. She and her colleagues reviewed existing research and conducted original work to understand how diversity influences student learning and democracy outcomes. Professor Gurin testified that research substantiates the claim that a diverse university environment stimulates students to be more actively engaged in the learning process and leads to the following positive learning outcomes:

- growth in active thinking processes that reflect a more complex, less automatic mode of thought,
- engagement and motivation,
- learning of a broad range of intellectual and academic skills, and
- greater value placed on these skills in the post-college years.

In addition, Professor Gurin argued for democracy outcomes such that students educated in diverse institutions are more motivated and better suited to participate in an increasingly heterogeneous and complex society. To participate effectively, students have to (1) learn to understand and consider the multiple perspectives that are inherent in a diverse environment; (2) deal with the conflicts that different perspectives sometimes entail; and (3) appreciate the common values and integrative forces that incorporate these differences in the pursuit of the broader common good. The democracy outcomes relate to these factors:

CITIZENSHIP ENGAGEMENT Citizenship engagement is the motivation to participate in activities that affect society and the political structure, as well as actual participation in community service in the five years following college. Students also demonstrate an understanding of how others think about issues, what is commonly called "perspective-taking" in cognitive psychology.

RACIAL/CULTURAL ENGAGEMENT Racial/cultural engagement includes cultural knowledge and awareness, as well as motivation to participate in activities that promote racial understanding.

COMPATIBILITY OF DIFFERENCES Compatibility of differences encompasses students' belief that basic values are common across racial and ethnic groups, their understanding of the potentially constructive aspects of group conflict, and their belief that differences are not inevitably divisive to the social fabric of society.

Professor Gurin also found that students who participated in a diverse curriculum were more likely to have interracial contact through friendships, neighborhoods, and work settings after college. They also felt that their college years had well prepared them for graduate school and for jobs after college.

Transcommunality

Transculturation is occurring not only between Chicanos and whites, but also between Chicanos and other ethnic and racial groups. In a political move to coalesce for mobilization around social justice issues, different ethnic and racial groups have adopted the label "people of Color" to name their informal "rainbow coalition." Specifically, "people of Color" refers to Chicanos/as, Asians, Native Americans, and Blacks, all of whom are U.S. minorities. Proponents capitalize "Color" to signify that it refers to specific ethnic groups. "Black" is also capitalized following the argument that it refers not merely to skin pigmentation but also to a "heritage, an experience, a cultural and **personal identity,** the meaning of which becomes specifically stigmatic and/or glorious and/or ordinary under specific social conditions. It is socially created as, and at least in the American context is no less specifically meaningful or definitive than, any linguistic, tribal, or religious ethnicity, all of which are conventionally recognized by capitalization" (Mackinnon 1982, 516). On the other hand, "white" is often left lowercased because it does not refer to specific or a cluster of ethnic groups but to many. This opening up of labels to name identifications "in the making" has created more room for previously derogated groups to explore their identities and claim them as positive affirmations of self—whether biracial, multiracial, feminist, lesbian, gay, or physically challenged (among others).

People of Color reclaiming the power to name themselves has also facilitated creating what sociologist John Brown Childs calls **transcommunality.** According to Brown Childs (1994, 49), transcommunality is the highest level of multiculturalism; he defines it as the ability of individuals to communicate and work across ethnic and racial lines without obliterating their own ethnic and racial distinctiveness. As an example, he cites the successful Justice "Gang Truce" Summit that met in Kansas City in 1993. The summit brought together gang members, community activists, and spiritual leaders from Latino/a, African American, and indigenous communities, with the goal of promoting peace and justice across ethnic and racial lines. Similarly, Chicanas'/os' greater awareness of their common fate with other subordinate groups has increased their willingness to create coalitions with African Americans, Asians, and Native American peoples.

■ Summary

In this chapter we reviewed the most recent sociodemographic and economic changes that are increasing the process of globalization and how these changes influence the formation of new social identities. Following are the major points of the chapter.

- Increasing globalization is expanding the amount of contact that individuals residing in the United States have with Mexico. The "border" is becoming more permeable, at least for legal U.S. residents, as people move between the two countries with more ease than in previous times.

- Coupled with greater globalization is a dramatic increase in the numbers of Latinos/as in the United States. This numerical increase is beginning to be felt in state and national elections, with the 2000 elections marking significant milestones in Latinos'/as' participation in electoral politics.

- Latinos/as, as a group, have frequent and intense contact with their countries of origin and are more likely to maintain their language and cultural ties and less likely to become assimilated.

- Increasing acceptance of multiculturalism, as well as increases in the numbers of ethnically and racially diverse individuals, have led to multiple group cultural adaptations to their social identity memberships.

- Increasing globalization and the greater number of Latinos/as and other people of Color in the United States have resulted in more white people becoming transculturated. That is, white people are beginning to acquire Spanish language ability and Mexican cultural knowledge that allow them to navigate between different cultural worlds.

- The most recent research on multiculturalism is beginning to document the importance of a diverse education and participation in diverse social environments in the development of white students' definition of citizenship and participation in a democratic society.

- People of Color are also creating coalitions to fight for social justice through the process of transcommunality.

These are exciting times for young people who are considering becoming the next generation of writers and scholars in the social sciences. Social science as we know it is about to be transformed not only by the internal development of theory and research, but also by the social and cultural transformations taking place in society. This is the first time in history when power, as determined through voting in electoral politics, will shift significantly from a white majority to a multicultural plurality. Academic writers will be charged with the task of charting this course of events and aiding the transition to a more truly democratic and participatory society.

■ Discussion Exercises

1. On a piece of paper write twenty statements answering the question "Who am I?"

2. Next, in order of importance, write down five groups you feel you belong to.

3. Exchange your answers with another student and ask that person three questions that will allow you to get to know him or her better as a person. Then allow him or her to ask you three questions as well.

4. Next each of you writes a short paragraph introducing your partner to another person, incorporating all that you learned about him or her.

5. Read the paragraph aloud to your partner and ask if he or she thinks your paragraph is an accurate description. Why or why not? What would your partner modify? Repeat the same process with the paragraph your partner wrote about you.

■ Note

1. The North American Free Trade Agreement (NAFTA) went into effect on January 1, 1994, creating the largest free trade area in the world between Canada, Mexico, and the United States. The results of the agreement have been mixed. Supporters feel that it has strengthened the economies of all three countries, while critics feel that environmental laws are often violated, workers in the United States have lost jobs, and Mexican workers have not enjoyed the protections extended to U.S. workers. For more information see http://www.citizen.org/trade/nafta.

◼ GLOSSARY

acculturation: The degree to which minority ethnic or racial groups adopt white mainstream values and customs.

aprendí ser fuerte: I learned to be strong.

assimilation: The process by which a minority group becomes like the majority group. Generally, assimilation implies the loss of the minority group's cultural characteristics.

Chicano Movement: The political movement of the 1960s and 1970s that emphasized the building of Chicano identity based on Mexican Americans' neglected history in this country as well as economic justice.

chongo: Hair bun.

chuca: *see* pachuca.

cognitive alternatives: Perceived alternatives to negotiating the existing power differential between groups in society.

colegio es para los ricos: School is for the rich.

consciousness: An individual's awareness of where in the status hierarchies his or her group memberships lie in comparison to other social groups in society (Gurin, Miller, and Gurin 1980).

consensually dominant group: A group that is valued in society and therefore has unproblematic social identities because its members do not suffer from stigma. Tajfel (1981) suggests a consensually dominant group's social identities are so natural as to be almost invisible (e.g., white, male, heterosexual, and wealthy).

consensually subordinate group: A group that is not valued in society; individuals who belong to such a group have to negotiate the stigma attached to their social identities.

degrouping: According to Apfelbaum (1979), *degrouping* is accomplished by taking away a subordinate group's language, culture, and worldview. Dominants take away any tools that would help subordinates develop independent standards and lead them to question the universal rule (*see also* regrouping).

Día de los Muertos: (Day of the Dead), also referred to as All Saints' Day and All Souls' Day, is celebrated in all Catholic countries, with the biggest celebrations occurring in Mexico. The celebration begins on the evening of October 31 and continues until November 2. The purpose is to remember family members who have passed away. According to popular belief, their souls return during this two-day celebration to enjoy the gifts and flowers placed on their gravesites. Families also construct altars in their homes with deceased family members' favorite foods, photographs, and other objects. (For more information, search the Internet for "Day of the Dead.")

dolor: Physical or emotional pain.

empowerment: The process of increasing personal, interpersonal, or political power so that individuals can take action to improve their life situation (Gutiérrez 1990). It involves four psychological changes: (1) increasing self-efficacy, (2) developing group consciousness, (3) reducing self-blame, and (4) assuming personal responsibility for change.

ese libro que parece que nunca va a terminar: That book that it seems she's never going to finish.

gender: The meanings that society and individuals attach to being female or male (e.g., females are emotional and males are tough).

identification: The degree to which individuals are aware of, and attach positive emotional significance to, belonging to one or more social groups.

internal colonial model: The reinterpretation of the history of Mexican descendants in the United States as that of a colonized group, rather than an immigrant group. This history of colonization of the Southwest is the distinguishing characteristic of Chicanos' negotiation of their identity in this country and gives them commonalties with other colonized groups like Native Americans and Blacks.

La Migra: Mexican slang for the Immigration and Naturalization Service officers who parole and oversee the border between Mexico and the United States.

Latina/o: A person who is a native or inhabitant of Western Hemisphere countries south of the United States, including Mexico and the countries in Central and South America and the Caribbean. The term also applies to a person living in the United States who comes from, or whose ancestors come from, one of these countries.

Lucha: Nickname for Alicia.

meritocracy: The social structure of Western democracies, based on a concept that individuals can achieve status in society through their accomplishments rather than by birthright (*see also* universal rule).

mestizaje: The process of racial and cultural mixture between Spaniards, Indians, and to a lesser extent Blacks, which occurred following the colonization of Mexico.

mestizo: A Spanish term for someone of mixed race. Mexicans have a mixed racial and ethnic heritage that includes elements of Spanish, Indian, European, and African ancestries, among others.

mi cuerpo: My body.

mi primer educación: My first education, my first time going to school.

mi raza: My race. *Raza* commonly refers to *la raza Latina*, or the Latino/a people in the United States. La Raza symbolizes the claiming of solidarity and identification among all Latino/a groups living in the United States.

mis hijos: My sons and daughters.

nomás no había dinero: There was no money.

otra mujer: The other woman; the mistress of a married man.

pachuca: Female gang member.

people of Color: A term for nonwhite groups who are subordinated and underrepresented in U.S. society. It commonly refers to Chicanos/as, Latinos/as, Blacks, Asians, and Native Americans.

personal identity: The aspect of self composed of psychological traits and dispositions that gives an individual personal uniqueness.

psychological work: Cognitive and emotional work which members of low-status groups must undergo to achieve a positive sense of distinctiveness and feel good about the groups they belong to (Tajfel 1981).

¿Qué te crees tú?: Who do you think you are?

¿Quién soy yo?: Who am I?

¿Quiénes somos?: Who are we?

¿Quiénes son?: Who are they?

regrouping: The process of a degrouped group reacquiring its history, language, and culture in order to feel the strength and beauty of their group memberships (*see also* degrouping).

self-efficacy: A belief in one's ability to plan and execute the courses of action required to produce a given outcome; a feeling of confidence and competence (Bandura 1997).

sex: The biological status of being male or female (*see also* gender).

social categorization: The process of associating people with groups based on their common attributes. Nationality, language, race, ethnicity, skin color, or any other social or physical characteristic can be the basis for social categorization and thus the foundation for the creation of social identities.

social comparison: The process of evaluating one's thoughts and actions by comparing them to those of others in the environment. The characteristics of the groups one belongs to, such as their status or relative wealth, achieve significance in relation to perceived differences from other groups and the value connotations of those differences.

social engagement model: A framework for studying behavior that assumes that all individuals have subjective definitions of their social engagement in their life spaces. Individuals actively engage in defining their life space in any sphere of social involvement.

social identity: The aspects of an individual's self-identity that derive from his or her knowledge of being a member of categories and groups or people, along with the value and emotional significance attached to those memberships.

socialization practices: The norms and practices that parents follow in raising their children and that shape the children's identity.

solo mexicana: The only Mexican woman in the place.

soy la mujer: I am the woman.

subjective definitions: Personal perceptions of social experiences, which may vary from individual to individual or from group to group.

tienes que ser fuerte. Como las meras mujeres: You have to be strong like real women.

toda la gente: All the people.

"Todos los hombres son iguales. Me voy a vengar de todos los hombres," decía mi mamá: "Men are all the same. I'm going to get revenge on all men," my mother used to say.

tokenism: One of the mechanisms dominant groups use to oppress subordinate groups by allowing only a few individuals from the subordinate group access to privilege (Apfelbaum 1979). Successful subordinate group members are used as examples to be followed by members of their group and to further reinforce the ideology of meritocracy (*see also* meritocracy).

transcommunality: The highest level of multiculturalism; the condition in which individuals can communicate and work across ethnic and racial lines without obliterating their own ethnic and racial distinctiveness (Childs 1994).

transculturation: An individual's ability to function at some level in the social life of a different cultural group than his or her own, while still maintaining his or her own cultural social life.

transnationalism: The development of social identities based on the connection or maintenance of ties to the individual's country of origin as well as to the country he or she is presently living in.

una escuelita: A little school.

una noche: One night.

universal rule: A universally defined set of conditions for success in a meritocracy. The universal rule supposedly applies equally to all individuals in society, but in reality those from privileged groups have preferential access to the skills and advantages necessary to perform according to the universal rule (*see also* meritocracy).

violencia: Violence.

y un día: And one day.

BIBLIOGRAPHY

Almaguer, Tomás. 1974. Historical notes on Chicano oppression: The dialectics of racial and class domination in North America. *Aztlán* 5 (1–2): 27–56.

Alvarez, Rodolfo. 1973. The psycho-historical and socioeconomic development of the Chicano community in the United States. *Social Science Quarterly* 53: 920–42.

Anzaldúa, Gloria. 1990. *Making face, making soul/haciendo caras: Creative and critical perspectives by feminists of color.* San Francisco: Aunt Lute Press.

Apfelbaum, Erika. 1979. Relations of domination and movements for liberation: An analysis of power between groups. In *The social psychology of intergroup relations,* ed. William G. Austin and Stephen Worchel, 188–204. Monterey, Calif.: Brooks/Cole.

——. 1999. Twenty years later. *Feminism and Psychology* 9 (3): 300–7.

Baca Zinn, Maxine. 1995. Social science theorizing for Latino families in the age of diversity. In *Understanding Latino families: Scholarship, policy, and practice,* ed. Ruth E. Zambrana, 177–89. Thousand Oaks, Calif.: Sage Publications.

Bandura, Albert. 1997. *Self-efficacy: The exercise of control.* New York: W. H. Freeman and Co.

Becker, Howard S. 1963. *Outsiders: Studies in the sociology of deviance.* New York: Free Press.

Blauner, Robert. 1972. *Racial oppression in America.* New York: Harper and Row.

Bridges, Judith S. 1993. Pink or blue: Gender-stereotypic perceptions of infants as conveyed by birth congratulations cards. *Psychology of Women Quarterly* 17 (2): 193–206.

Brown Childs, J. 1994. The value of transcommunal identity politics. *Z Magazine* 7 (7–8): 48–51.

Castillo, Ana. 1995. *Massacre of the dreamers.* New York: Plume Books.

Chronis, Peter G. 1998. Salazar makes history: Coloradan is first Hispanic in statewide office. *Denver Post,* Nov. 8, p. A-19.

Cohen, Katherine. 2002. *The truth about getting in: A top college advisor tells you everything you need to know.* New York: Hyperion Books.

Crenshaw, Kimberle. 1993. Demarginalizing the intersection of race and sex: A black feminist critique of anti-discrimination doctrine, feminist theory, and anti-racist politics. In *Feminist legal theory: Foundations,* ed. D. Kelly Weisberg, 383–95. Philadelphia: Temple University Press.

Cuádraz, Gloria H. 1996. Experiences of multiple marginality: A case study of Chicana "scholarship women." In *Racial and ethnic diversity in higher education. ASHE reader series,* ed. Caroline Turner, Mildred García, Amauri Nora, and Laura Rendón, 210–22. Needham Heights, Mass.: Simon and Schuster Custom Publishing.

Cuádraz, Gloria H., and Jennifer Pierce. 1994. From scholarship girls to scholarship women: Surviving the contradictions of class and race in academe. *Explorations in Ethnic Studies* 17: 210–22.

Fine, Michelle, Lois Weis, Linda C. Powell, and L. Mun Wong, eds. 1997. *Off white: Readings on society, race and culture.* New York: Routledge.

Fiol-Matta, Liza. 2001. Beyond survival: A politics/poetics of Puerto Rican consciousness. In *Telling to live: Latina feminist testimonios,* ed. The Latina Feminist Group, 148–55. Durham and London: Duke University Press.

Franzoi, Stephen L. 1996. *Social psychology.* Madison, Wis.: Brown and Benchmark Publishers.

Freire, Paulo. 1970. *Pedagogy of the oppressed.* New York: The Continuum Publishing Corp.

García, Eugene E., and Aída Hurtado. 1995. Becoming American: A review of current research on the development of racial and ethnic identity in children. In *Toward a common destiny: Improving race and ethnic relations in America,* ed. Willis D. Hawley and Anthony Wells Jackson, 163–84. San Francisco: Jossey-Bass Inc.

Gaspar de Alba, Alicia. 1998. *Chicano art inside/outside the master's house: Cultural politics and the CARA exhibition.* Austin: University of Texas Press.

Gibbs, Nancy. 2001. The new frontier/*La nueva frontera:* A whole new world. *Time,* June 11, 38–45.

Goffman, Erving. 1987. *Gender advertisements.* New York: Harper and Row.

Goldberger, Nancy, Jill Tarule, Blythe Clinchy, and Mary Belenky, eds. 1996. *Knowledge, difference and power: Essays inspired by women's ways of knowing.* New York: Basic Books.

Gonzales, Patrisia, and Roberto Rodriguez. 2002. I.N.S. Disbands, Census eliminates "Hispanic" category. *Column of the Americas,* March 29. Available from http://www.uexpress.com/columnoftheamericas/?uc_full_date=20020329. (Last accessed August 8, 2003.)

González, Arturo. 2002. *Mexican Americans in the U.S. economy: Quest for buenos días.* Tucson: University of Arizona Press.

Gordon, Milton. 1964. *Assimilation in American life: The role of race, religion, and national origin.* New York: Oxford University Press.

Gould, Stephen J. 1996. *Full house: The spread of excellence from Plato to Darwin.* New York: Harmony Books.

Gurin, Patricia, Aída Hurtado, and Tim Peng. 1994. Group contacts and ethnicity in the social identities of Mexicanos and Chicanos. *Personality and Social Psychology Bulletin* 20 (5): 521–32.

Gurin, Patricia, Arthur H. Miller, and Gerald Gurin. 1980. Stratum identification and consciousness. *Social Psychology Quarterly* 43 (1): 30–47.

Gutiérrez, Lorraine. 1990. Working with women of color: An empowerment perspective. *Social Work* 35 (2): 149–53.

Haney, Craig, and Philip Zimbardo. 1998. The past and future of U.S. prison policy: Twenty-five years after the Stanford prison experiment. *American Psychologist* 53 (7): 709–27.

Harris, Angela P. 1990. Race and essentialism in feminist legal theory. *Stanford Law Review* 42: 581–616.

Harris, Cheryl I. 1993. Whiteness as property. *Harvard Law Review* 106 (8): 1709–91.

Hinojosa, María. 2001. Living la vida Latina. *Time,* June 11, p. 79.

hooks, bell. 1989. *Talking back: Thinking feminist, thinking black.* Boston: South End Press.

Hurtado, Aída. 1994. Community assessment Starlight Elementary: Final report. Unpublished manuscript. University of California, Santa Cruz.

———. 1995. Variations, combinations, and evolutions: Latino families in the United States. In *Understanding Latino families: Scholarship, policy, and practice,* ed. Ruth E. Zambrana, 40–61. Thousand Oaks, Calif.: Sage Publications.

———. 1996. Strategic suspensions: Feminists of color theorize the production of knowledge. In *Knowledge, difference, and power: Essays inspired by women's ways of knowing,* ed. Nancy Goldberger, with Mary Belenky, Blythe Clinchy, and Jill Tarule, 372–92. New York: Basic Books.

———. 1997. Understanding multiple group identities: Inserting women into cultural transformations. *Journal of Social Issues* 53 (2): 299–327.

Hurtado, Aída, and Carlos Arce. 1987. Mexicans, Chicanos, Mexican Americans, or Pochos . . . ¿Que somos? *Aztlán* 17 (1): 103–29.

Hurtado, Aída, Patricia Gurin, and Tim Peng. 1994. Social identities—A framework for studying the adaptations of immigrants and ethnics: Mexicans in the United States. *Social Problems* 41(1): 129–51.

Hurtado, Aída, Jaclyn Rodríguez, Patricia Gurin, and Janette Beals. 1993. The impact of Mexican descendants' social identity on the ethnic socialization of children. In *Ethnic identity: Formation and transmission among Hispanics and other minorities,* ed. Marta E. Bernal and George P. Knight, 131–62. New York: SUNY Press.

Hurtado, Aída, and Raúl Rodríguez. 1989. Language as a social problem: The repression of Spanish in south Texas. *Journal of Multilingual and Multicultural Development* 10 (5): 401–19.

Hurtado, Aída, and Abigail J. Stewart. 1997. Through the looking glass: Implications of studying whiteness for feminist methods. In *Off white: Readings on society, race, and culture,* ed. Michelle Fine, Linda Powell, Lois Weis, and L. Mun Wong, 297–311. New York: Routledge.

Latina Feminist Group. 2001. *Telling to live: Latina feminist testimonies.* Durham and London: Duke University Press.

Lewin, Kurt. 1948. *Resolving social conflicts: Selected papers on group dynamics, 1935–1946,* ed. Gertrud Weiss. New York: Harper and Brothers.

López, David, and Yen Espíritu. 1990. Panethnicity in the United States: A theoretical framework. *Ethnic and Racial Studies* 13 (2):198–224.

Mackinnon, Catherine. 1982. Feminism, Marxism, method, and the state: An agenda for the theory. *Signs: Journal of Women in Culture and Society* 7 (31): 515–44.

Meléndez, Claudia S. 2002. Conflicts of two cultures alter Mexican-American singer's ego. *San Jose Mercury News* April 9, 1E.

Moya, Paula M. 2002. *Learning from experience: Minority identities, multicultural struggles.* Berkeley: University of California Press.

Park, Robert E., and Ernest Burgess. 1921. *Introduction to the science of sociology.* Chicago: University of Chicago Press.

Parties divide up statewide offices: Bustamante leads Leslie in lt. governor race. 1998. *Santa Cruz Sentinel,* November, p. C-2.

Pérez, Emma. 1991. Sexuality and discourse: Notes from a Chicana survivor. In *Chicana lesbians: The girls our mothers warned us about,* ed. Carla Trujillo, 159–84. Berkeley: Third Woman Press.

Phinney, Jean S. 1996. When we talk about American ethnic groups, what do we mean? *American Psychologist* 51 (9): 918–27.

Portillo, Lourdes, and Sylvia Muñoz, directors. 1990. *La ofrenda: The day of the dead* [Film]. San Francisco: Xochitl Films.

Redfield, Robert, Ralph Linton, and Melville J. Herskovits. 1936. Memorandum for the study of acculturation. *American Anthropologist* 38 (1): 149–52.

Rendón, Laura I. 1992. From the barrio to the academy: Revelations of a Mexican American "scholarship girl." *New Directions in Community Colleges* 90 (Winter): 55–64.

——. 2000. Academics of the heart: Reconnecting the scientific mind with the spirit's artistry. *Review of Higher Education* 24 (1): 1–13.

Roa, Jessica. 2003. Reclamation. In *Voicing Chicana feminisms: Young women speak out on sexuality and identity,* by Aída Hurtado. New York: New York University Press.

Saldívar-Hull, Sonia. 2000. *Feminism on the border: Chicana gender politics and literature.* Berkeley and Los Angeles: University of California Press.

Sánchez, Elba. 2003. Cartohistografía: Continente de una voz/Cartohistography: One voice's continent. In *Chicana feminisms: A critical reader,* ed. Gabriela Arredondo, Aída Hurtado, Norma Klahn, Olga Nájera-Ramírez, and Patricia Zavella. Durham and London: Duke University Press.

Sandoval, Chela. 1991. U.S. third world feminism: The theory and method of oppositional consciousness in the postmodern world. *Genders* 10 (Spring): 1–24.

Serros, Michelle. 1993. *Chicana falsa and other stories of death, identity, and Oxnard.* New York: Riverhead Books.

State Democrats retain edge in House Races. 1998. *Santa Cruz Sentinel,* November, p. C-2.

Steinhorn, Leonard, and Barbara Diggs-Brown. 2000. *By the color of our skin: The illusion of integration.* New York: Plume Books.

Tajfel, Henri. 1978. *Differentiation between social groups: Studies in the social psychology of intergroup relations.* London: Academic Press.

———. 1981. *Human groups and social categories: Studies in social psychology.* London: Cambridge University Press.

Tello, Jerry. 1994. Cara y Corazón, Face and Heart: A family-strengthening, rebalancing and community mobilization process. San Antonio, TX: National Latino Children's Institute.

Thomas, Cathy Booth. 2001. The rise of the NAFTA manager. *Time,* June 11, p. 53.

Tumulty, Karen. 2001. Courting a sleeping giant: The biggest U.S. minority group, Hispanics, have yet to flex their political muscle. *Time,* June 11, p. 74.

Zavella, Patricia. 1987. *Women's work and Chicano families: Workers of the Santa Clara Valley.* Ithaca, N.Y.: Cornell University Press.

■ SOURCE CREDITS

Introduction

Laura Rendón, "Quién soy yo," from "Academics of the Heart: Reconnecting the Scientific Mind with the Spirit's Artistry," *The Review of Higher Education* 24, no. 1 (2000), 1–13. © The Association for the Study of Higher Education. Reprinted with permission of The Johns Hopkins University Press.

Chapter 1

Figure 1 courtesy of María Hurtado.

Figures 2 and 3 and Topic Highlights 1–5 were previously published in Hurtado, Aída. 1997. "Understanding multiple group identities: Inserting women into cultural transformations," *Journal of Social Issues* 53(2): 299–327; reprinted courtesy of Blackwell Publishers.

"A Day with Alejandro," reprinted with permission from the National Latino Children's Institute, Cara y Corazón Curriculum.

Figure 6 photo by Aída Hurtado.

Chapter 2

"My Altar," by Marisol Lorenzana, included courtesy of the author.

Figure 6 photographed by Aída Hurtado.

Figure 7 "An Ofrenda for Dolores del Rio, 1984; Reconstructed 1990," from the collection of the National Museum of American Art of the Smithsonian. Reprinted by permission.

"Disco Gymnasium" and "What Is Bad" by Michele Serros, from *Chicana Falsa: And Other Stories of Death, Identity, and Oxnard* (reprinted by Riverhead Books, 1998). Used by permission of Michele Serros.

Topic Highlight 6, "Reflections on My Altar," by Yvonne Miller, included courtesy of the author.

Figure 9 previously appeared in Judith S. Bridges, "Pink or blue: Gender-stereotypic perceptions of infants as conveyed by birth congratulations cards," *Psychology of Women Quarterly* 17 (1993): 193–205. Reprinted by permission of Blackwell Publishing.

Topic Highlight 7, "Mi Altar," by Emma, included courtesy of the author.

Topic Highlight 8, "Untitled," by Kristin Tillim, included courtesy of the author.

Excerpts from *Mi Familia* copyright © 1995, New Line Productions, Inc. All rights reserved. Dialogue reprinted courtesy of New Line Productions, Inc.

"Altar Response," by Xochitl Gutierrez, included courtesy of the author.

Chapter 3

Table 1, "Analysis of data collected during the 1998–99 school year regarding Northern California high schools and availability of Advanced Placement courses for minority students." © ACLU Foundation of Southern California. Used by permission.

Topic Highlight 16, Ray Hartmann, "Blinded by the White: We Caucasians Would Prefer to Ignore Our Preferences," *Riverfront Times* (St. Louis), February 5, 1998. Reprinted by permission.

Topic Highlight 17, Scott Smallwood, "New Study at MIT Finds That Female Faculty Members Still Feel Marginalized," *Chronicle of Higher Education,* March 20, 2002. © 2002, *The Chronicle of Higher Education.* Reprinted by permission.

Topic Highlight 19, "Reclamation," by Jessica Roa, from *Voicing Chicana feminisms: Young women speak out on sexuality and identity,* by Aída Hurtado (New York: New York University Press, 2003). Reprinted by permission.

Topic Highlight 20, "Hisss Panics," by Elba Sánchez, from *When Skin Peels,* a spoken-word CD by Elba Sánchez and Olga Angelina García (Calaca Press, 2000). Used by permission.

Topic Highlight 21, Patrisia Gonzales and Roberto Rodriguez, "I.N.S. Disbands, Census Eliminates 'Hispanic' Category," Gonzales/Rodriguez write the syndicated Column of the Americas for Universal Press Syndicate.

Topic Highlight 23, "Conflicts of Two Cultures Alter Mexican-American Singer's Ego" (April 9, 2002), by Claudia S. Meléndez. Copyright © *San Jose Mercury News,* All rights reserved. Reproduced with permission.

Figure 11, *Tamalada (Making Tamales)* © 1988 by Carmen Lomas Garza (oil on linen mounted on wood, 24 x 32 inches). Photo credit: Wolfgang Dietze. From the collection of Paula Maciel-Benecke and Norbert Benecke, Aptos, California. Used by permission.

Figure 12, *Posada (Inn)* © 1987 by Carmen Lomas Garza (gouache, 20 x 28 inches). Photo credit: Wolfgang Dietze. From the collection of Marina D. Alvarado and Gilbert Mercado Jr., Whittier, California. Used by permission.

Figure 13, *Homenaje a Frida Kahlo* © 1978 by Yreina D. Cervántez—Xicana artist (watercolor). Used by permission.

Chapter 4

Figure 14, "Amexica,"*Time,* June 11, 2001, vol. 57, no. 123. © 2001 TIME Inc. Reprinted by permission.

Topic Highlight 25, "Two Hometowns/Bay Area's Second-Generation Mexican Immigrants Advance While Keeping One Foot in the World of Their Parents," by

Louis Freedberg. Copyright © 2002 by the *San Francisco Chronicle*. Reproduced with permission of the *San Francisco Chronicle* in the format Other Book via Copyright Clearance Center.

Figure 18, "The Border Is Everywhere," *Time,* June 11, 2001. © 2001 TIME Inc. Reprinted by permission.

INDEX

acculturate, 19

acculturated, 9, 11

acculturation, 6, 7, 9, 10, 11, 13, 23, 24, 63, 113, 123

affirmative action, 91, 95, 124

African American blood, 13; community, 70

African Americans, 9, 12, 19, 77, 91, 99, 111, 126

African roots, 92

Albuquerque, 104

Almaguer, Tomás, 13

altar, 42, 44

Alvarez, Rodolfo, 84, 88, 89, 109

Americanization, 7, 24; policies, 93

Americanos, 98

Amexica, 109

Anzaldúa, Gloria, 100, 112, 113

Apfelbaum, Erika, 68, 69, 70, 73, 76, 79, 81, 83, 91, 105, 106, 107

Argentines, 117

Asian American, 19, 91

Asians, 9, 125, 126

assimilation, 6, 7, 9, 10, 11, 13, 19, 23, 24, 59, 63, 68, 92, 110, 112, 113; and acculturation framework, 16–17, 19, 20, 21, 22, 24; and acculturation model, 25; framework, 11

Aztlán, 90

Bandura, Albert, 83

Becker, Howard Saul, 43

bell hooks, 112

Black people, 83

Blacks, 125

Blauner, Robert, 13

Boricua, 92

Bustamante, Cruz, 111

California, 13, 17, 70, 109, 111, 115

Californiano/a, 92

Cara y Corazón (face and heart) workshop, 3, 5, 6, 24

cargas y regalos (burdens and gifts), 4

Castillo, Ana, 113

Central America, 59

Cervántez, Yreina D., 101

Chicago, 89, 115, 117

Chicano/a parents, 4, 6, 7, 17, 18, 19, 20

Chicano Art: Resistance and Affirmation (CARA) exhibition, 101

Chicano: experience, 91; Generation, 90; Movement, 10, 91; Studies, 91

children of Color, 82

Childs, John Brown, 126

Chilean, 117

Chronis, Peter, 111

citizenship engagement, 125

Civil Rights Commission, 93

class, 6, 15, 24, 35, 43, 44, 45, 69

cognitive, 64; alternatives, 57, 59, 84

colonization, 12

Colorado, 111

compatibility of differences, 125

concientizatción, 113

conscious, 50

consciousness, 50, 51, 57, 59, 63, 64, 84, 92

consensually dominant, 43; subordinant groups, 43

corridos, 105

Creation Generation, 90

Crenshaw, Kimberle, 112

Cuádraz, Gloria, 113; and Jennifer Pierce, 113

Cubans, 117

cultural adaptation, 13, 22, 23, 24, 112,

cultural adaptation (*cont.*)
 113, 114; conflict, 13; diversity, 117;
 transformations, 13, 114

David (character in *Mi Familia*), 57, 63
definitional approach, 15
degrouping, 68, 73, 83, 105, 106, 107;
 process, 79
differential consciousness, 113
"Disco Gymnasium," 31–32, 35, 44
discrimination, 51, 81
dominant, 43
Dominicans, 117
Donna (character in "Disco Gymnasium"), 35
Downs, Lila, 99, 102–103

East Los Angeles, 59
El Día de los Muertos (The Day of the
 Dead), 104
Emma (*Mi Altar*), 44, 45, 46–47
empowerment, 73, 79, 82, 83, 84, 107
engagement, 24
English, 18
English-only legislation, 95
establishment of the universal rule, 68
ethnic, 12, 13, 22, 23, 125
ethnic cultural maintenance, 23
ethnic distinctiveness, 126
ethnic group, 23, 63
ethnic identification, 22, 91
ethnic identity, 7, 9, 12, 24, 51
ethnicity, 6, 10, 15, 16, 20, 21, 22, 24, 35,
 37, 43, 45, 64, 69, 73, 112, 113, 115
ethnic labeling, 91, 92, 93
ethnic socialization, 119
ethnic studies, 12, 13

feminist, 126; movement, 11
feminists, 12, 91
Fine, Michelle, 45

Fiol-Matta, Liza, 100
Franzoi, Stephen, 40, 43
Friere, Paolo, 84

García, Eugene: and Aída Hurtado, 7,
 93
Garza, Carmen Lomas, 101, 104–105
Gaspar de Alba, Alicia, 101, 104
gender, 6, 9, 10, 11, 13, 15, 20, 24, 35,
 40, 42, 43, 44, 45, 64, 69, 77, 92
Gibbs, Nancy, 109
globalization, 117, 126, 127
Goffman, Erving, 40
Goldberg, Whoopi, 77, 79, 82, 83; char-
 acter played by, 82, 83
Goldberger, Nancy, 112
Gómez-Peña, Guillermo, 100
Gonzales, Patrisia, 92, 96–98
Gonzalez, Antonio, 111
González, Arturo, 50
Gordon, Milton, 6, 9
Gould, Stephen, 113
group empowerment, 79, 82
Guillermo ("Memo," character in *Mi
 Familia*), 59–63
Gurin, Patricia, 50, 51, 84, 124, 125;
 and Aída Hurtado, and Tim Peng,
 24, 44, 110
Gutiérrez, Lorraine, 82, 84–85

Haney, Craig: and Philip Zimbardo, 73
Harris, Cheryl, 71, 112
Hartmann, Ray, 71
Hernández, Rebecca, 119
Hinojosa, María, 117, 118, 119
Hispanic, 92, 96–98, 111, 112
Homenaje a Frida Kahlo (Homage to
 Frida Kahlo), 101
homophobia, 82
homosexual, 42
Hurtado, Aída, 9, 13, 17, 30; and

Abigail Stewart, 45, 71; and Carlos
  Arce, 93; and Patricia Gurin, and
  Timothy Peng, 91; and Raúl
  Rodríguez, 7, 93, 98; and Raúl
  Rodríguez, Patricia Gurin, and
  Jeanette Beals, 23, 24, 112
Hurtado, María, 3, 4, 5, 6

identification, 10, 50, 51, 57, 59, 89, 92,
  112
identity transformations, 115
immigrant, 18, 19, 21, 63, 87
immigrants, 3, 15, 22, 88, 92, 93, 109,
  112; Mexican, 109
immigration, 57
India, 69
Indígenas (Indians), 98
internal colonial model, 13, 24
intersex, 42

Jimmy (character in Mi Familia), 59, 63

language, 20
Latin America, 109
Latino/as, 22, 24, 57, 91, 92, 93, 99, 107,
  109, 110, 111, 112, 114, 117, 118, 119,
  126, 127; immigrants, 117; popula-
  tion, 111
Lewin, Kurt, 13, 15
life spaces, 13, 15, 22, 82, 85
López, David: and Yen Espíritu, 117
Lorenzana, Marisol, 27, 30, 42
Los Angeles, 51, 53, 59
lower class status, 89

Mackinon, Catherine, 126
Manito/a, 92
Massachusetts Institute of Technology
  (MIT), 77
master status, 43, 64
meritocracy, 68, 69, 73, 76, 107

Mesa-Bains, Amalia, 99
Mestiza consciousness, 113
Mestizaje, 95
Mestizos, 13
Mexicana, 117, 119
Mexican Americans, 88, 89, 91; Gener-
  ation, 89
Mexicanos, 98
Mexico, 3, 4, 15, 16, 17, 18, 24, 35, 44,
  50, 51, 53, 57, 59, 84, 87, 88, 89, 90,
  91, 106, 109, 111, 117, 123, 124, 126;
  art, 101; border, 111; culture, 90, 117,
  119; descendants, 91, 115; descent,
  89, 91; heritage, 91; immigrants, 111;
  migrants, 88
middle class, 45
Mi Familia/My Family, 51, 54–55, 63, 64
Miller, Yvonne, 37
Mojica, Claudia, 50
Moraga, Cherríe, 100, 112
Moya, Paula, 92
multiculturalism, 23, 112, 113, 123, 126,
  127
multiple identities, 30

Native Americans, 12, 125, 126
Nava, Gregory, 51
New York, 117
New York City, 119
Nicaraguan, 91
nongroup, 106
norteño music, 104

Oaxaca, 99
Oakland, 71

pan-ethnicity, 119
pan-ethnic label, 92
Park, Robert: and Ernest Burgess, 9
people of Color, 71, 73, 113, 125, 126,
  127

Pérez, Emma, 95, 98, 99
personal identity, 21, 30, 82, 126
personal responsibility, 84
Peruvians, 117
Phinney, Jean, 45, 112
physical ableness, 43, 64
physical challenges, 15, 44
"Pocho," 106
political action, 57
political empowerment, 68
Portillo, Lourdes: and Sylvia Muñoz, 99
psychological, 37; work, 43, 44
Puerto Ricans, 92, 117

race, 6, 9, 15, 20, 21, 24, 35, 37, 43, 44, 45, 64, 69, 77, 113
racial/cultural engagement, 125
racial distinctiveness, 126; diversity, 10; groups, 13, 22, 23; identity development, 77
racism, 82, 105
"rasquache," 106
rasquachismo, 104
Redfield, Robert: and Ralph Linton, and Melville Herskovits, 123
regalos, 24
regional identities, 92
regrouping, 79, 105
Rendón, Laura, 113, 114
Rivera, Diego, 101
Roa, Jessica, 69, 70, 73, 81, 93
Rodriguez, Roberto, 92, 96–98

Salazar, Ken, 111
Saldívar-Hull, Sonia, 98
Salvadoran, 91–92, 117
Sánchez, Antonia, 57, 59, 63
Sánchez, Chucho, 57, 63
Sánchez, Elba, 92, 94–95
Sánchez, José and María, 51, 53

Sánchez, Loretta, 111
Sánchez, Memo, 59–63
Sánchez family, 51
Sandoval, Chela, 112, 113
self-efficacy, 83, 85
self identity, 30
Serros, Michelle, 30, 32, 84
sex, 40, 42
sexism, 82
sexual identification, 24; orientation, 43, 64
sexuality, 15, 42, 44
skin color, 37, 64
social adaptations, 63, 112
social categorization, 37, 42, 43, 64
social class, 20, 35, 64
social comparison, 37, 42, 43, 51, 64, 115
social engagement, 13
social engagement model, 13, 15, 16–17, 20, 22, 24
social identification, 114, 119
social identity and identities, 15, 16, 21, 25, 30, 35, 36, 37, 42, 43, 44, 45, 50, 51, 59, 63, 64, 68, 81, 82, 84, 91, 98, 107, 113, 126
socialization, 21, 36; norms, 123; practices, 5
social psychologist, 13
Southwest Voter Registration Education Project, 111
"Spanglish," 106
Spanish, 7, 13, 18, 22, 25, 63, 92, 93, 95, 98, 99, 115, 124
Spanish-speaking parents, 18, 21
Steinhorn, Leonard: and Barbara Diggs-Brown, 77
stigma, 43, 57, 63, 64, 68, 81, 82, 84, 113
stigmatic, 126
stigmatized social identities, 84

Tajfel, Henri, 30, 37, 43, 44, 50, 51, 63, 68, 83, 91
Tejano/a, 92
Tello, Jerry, 3, 5, 6
Texas, 92, 93, 98, 115
"Tex-Mex," 106
Tillim, Kristin, 45
Time, 111, 112
tokenism, 76
tokens, 76, 77, 107
trait approach, 9
transcommunality, 125, 126, 127
transculturated, 124, 127
transculturation, 117, 123, 125
transgendered individuals, 42
transnational: identification, 123; identities, 117, 119, 123
transnationalism, 109
transvestites, 42

Treaty of Guadalupe Hidalgo, 84, 87
Tumulty, Karen, 111, 112

U.S. capitalism, 13
universal rule, 69, 70, 73, 106, 107
University of California, 71

Watsonville, California, 3, 4
West Coast, 92
white feminist movement, 11
Williams, Patricia, 112
women of Color, 11
women's movement, 90
working class, 45, 57, 98, 117
World War II, 12, 89

Zavella, Patricia, 13
Zinn, Baca 13

■ ABOUT THE AUTHORS

AÍDA HURTADO is professor of psychology at the University of California, Santa Cruz. Dr. Hurtado's research focuses on the effects of subordination on social identity and language. She is especially interested in group memberships like ethnicity, race, class, sexuality, and gender that are used to legitimize unequal distribution of power between groups. Dr. Hurtado's expertise is in survey methods with bilingual/bicultural populations. She has published on issues of language and social identity affecting the Mexican-origin population in the United States. Her most recent publications include *The Color of Privilege: Three Blasphemies on Race and Feminism* (University of Michigan Press, 1996); and *Voicing Chicana Feminisms: Young Women Speak Out on Sexuality and Identity* (New York University Press, 2003); *Chicana Feminisms: A Critical Reader* (coedited with Gabriela Arredondo, Norma Klahn, Olga Najera-Ramírez, and Patricia Zavella, Duke University Press, 2003). Dr. Hurtado received her B.A. in psychology and sociology from the University of Texas, Pan American, Edinburg, Texas, and her M.A. and Ph.D. in social psychology from the University of Michigan.

PATRICIA GURIN is professor of psychology and women's studies at the University of Michigan. Dr. Gurin's research focuses on intergroup relations, and she has published eight books and monographs, as well as numerous articles, examining how group memberships and identification affect the personal and social outcomes of various groups in American society, among them racial and ethnic groups, gender groups, age groups, and social-class groups. Much of her work has utilized national surveys conducted by the Institute for Social Research, where she has been a faculty associate since 1968. Since 1990–91, she has conducted research on student experiences with diversity at the University of Michigan. Professor Gurin was the main expert on behalf of the University of Michigan's Affirmative Action programs in the cases of *Gratz et al. v. Bollinger et al.* and *Grutter et al. v. Bollinger et al.* Her publications include *Black Consciousness, Identity, and Achievement* (coauthored with Edgar G. Epps); *Hope and Independence* (coauthored with James S. Jackson and Shirley Hatchett); and *Women, Politics and Change* (coedited with Louise Tilly).

Chicana/o Identity in a Changing U.S. Society is a volume in the series The Mexican American Experience, a cluster of modular texts designed to provide greater flexibility in undergraduate education. Each book deals with a single topic concerning the Mexican American population. Instructors can create a semester-length course from any combination of volumes, or may choose to use one or two volumes to complement other texts.

Additional volumes deal with the following subjects:

Mexican Americans and Health
Adela de la Torre and Antonio L. Estrada

Chicano Popular Culture
Charles M. Tatum

Mexican Americans and the U.S. Economy
Arturo González

Mexican Americans and the Law
Reynaldo Anaya Valencia, Sonia R. García, Henry Flores, and José Roberto Juárez Jr.

For more information, please visit
www.uapress.arizona.edu/textbooks/latino.htm